BREAKING FREE

A Guide to Achieving Personal and Professional
Freedom as a Lawyer

Gary Miles

Contents

Section 2: Keys to Freedom

Introduction

**What if the pressure of your practice was no longer so stressful?
What if you no longer felt burned out and overwhelmed?
What if you felt truly happy and fulfilled in your practice?**

You can make that happen. And you deserve that freedom. You face so much stress and pressure, don't you? Onerous billing requirements, obnoxious clients, challenging attorneys, demanding partners, a complex work environment, and stringent court calendars make our lives very stressful. In addition, there's intense competition among attorneys for a limited number of clients. And you get so consumed by the pressure of winning and obtaining a successful result for your clients.

Even though others may consider you successful, you often feel stuck, overwhelmed, and frustrated. This book is intended to help you free yourself from those pressures and achieve a level of success and happiness you did not think possible. What does it mean to free yourself, and why should you do it?

I have learned from years of experience that every one of us has some obstacle to our growth, something from our childhood, some experiences we have had, some habits that do not serve us, and some hindrances to our growth and development. Those obstacles hold us back. They restrain us. They prevent us from being everything we want to be and can be. More often than not, you're not even aware of them. They are part of our nature, our makeup. You need a better perception of how they are limiting you. Over the years, they have become part of who you are.

Because of them, you have developed behaviors that do not serve you. You have attitudes about yourself, what you're capable of, and, more importantly, what you're not. Those attitudes control us and prevent our progress. Resentments, fears, stress, and worry limit our happiness. These obstacles may create health problems, financial issues, and a lack of success. You feel trapped and overwhelmed.

I call these "prisons." It's as if you're locked up. You cannot free yourself. You cannot grow. You have lost your freedom to choose what you want to do and how you want to do it. Even worse than an actual prison, you're often unaware of how these limitations ensnare you. I will give you the keys to open your prisons.

This book is intended for lawyers who don't feel satisfied or happy in business or life. It will give you tools that will allow you to be successful and fulfilled in ways you never thought possible. It will help you to identify mental prisons that entrap you and then give you concrete, actionable steps on how to overcome every one of those obstacles.

While there are many things in life you don't have control over, you can control your thoughts, feelings, and actions. You can develop conscious ideas that serve you better and help you to become the person you want to be. People often look at their past, see how they've responded, see what they've not yet been able to accomplish, and conclude they cannot achieve more in the future. But when you change your thoughts and open your minds to new ways of thinking, feeling, and responding, you're freed from the hurdles previously limiting you.

You'll read about the obstacles that many of us have faced during our life. Not all of these will apply to you, but you'll quickly identify the ones that do. You'll learn about walls you must break through for a transformation and precisely how. You've worked hard to get where you are and deserve happiness and freedom.

This will be a journey of self-discovery and action. It won't be easy, and it will take work. But trust me, it will be worth it to you.

- Are you ready for this challenging journey?

- Will you accept the challenge of self-examination, of dispassionately reviewing yourself, who you are, what has happened to you, and how you react, to identify the prisons that cause problems for you?

- Are you willing to open yourself to a new way of thinking and reacting?

This will be a challenge, but it will be worth it. It will change your life. It will change your practice.

Let's get started!

How To Use This Book

This book will detail some of the most critical situations you often get trapped in. I call these the Twelve Prisons for apparent reasons.

The Twelve Prisons

1. Our Past
2. Overthinking the Future
3. Self-doubt and Imposter Syndrome
4. Burnout
5. Perfectionism
6. Stress
7. Fear
8. People Pleasing
9. Other People's Opinions
10. Comparison
11. Expectations
12. Limiting Beliefs

Most of us have been affected by each of them at some point. Probably all of us are affected by some of them right now. Each of these chapters is independent and self-contained. Generally, each chapter will fall into a similar pattern.

I will introduce the problem, explain what we will discuss in the chapter, describe the prison and how it affects us, detail the gifts of breaking out of that prison, and lay out specific tangible tools to free yourself from it. Some of the tools referred to will be used for more than one prison. For example, gratitude and acceptance are valuable tools for almost every negative emotion.

Because the chapters are independent, you do not have to read the entire book consecutively. You may pick any chapter to read separately from the others. You may skip ahead and go back to others. You may go back and revisit a chapter previously read. I encourage you, though, to learn from each chapter.

Use this book as a resource. When you have a day when self-doubt or perfectionism is more of a problem, for example, return to that chapter and read it. It will help. The tools inside are only as helpful as your effort. They require changes in your thoughts and your behaviors. To make them work, I encourage you to implement the tools. To make these changes, you must put forth the effort.

After the Twelve Prisons, you'll learn about the Twelve Keys to Freedom, each of which can unlock the doors behind which you find yourself stuck.

The Twelve Keys to Freedom

1. Acceptance
2. Gratitude
3. Living in the Present
4. Forgiveness
5. Mindfulness
6. Compassion
7. Authenticity
8. Emotional Intelligence
9. Growth Mindset
10. Law of Attraction

Please read each chapter and apply the tools daily to create a greater sense of personal freedom. I will describe the key, how it works, what gifts it provides, and a series of specific steps to start applying that key to freedom in your daily life.

If you trust the recommended tools, you can enjoy a sense of personal freedom that you have not yet experienced.

Here we go!

SECTION 1
Twelve Prisons

Prison 1: The Past

(Unearthing the Wounds of the Past: A Path to Lawyer Healing)

"Sooner or later, we've all got to let go of our past."
– Dan Brown

You've all had various experiences growing up. Some consider themselves to have had happy childhoods; others might feel their childhood was traumatic. Whether positive or negative or mixed, all these past influences impact your life and how you respond today. And unfortunately, the negative experiences may be limiting your current life.

The past affects us in four primary ways:

1. You may develop negative thoughts or limiting beliefs because of past experiences.

2. You may feel shame or guilt about something you never fixed.

3. Maybe you feel resentful about how someone treated you.

4. You might carry around regret over a professional choice or an opportunity you didn't pursue.

Not everyone is affected negatively, but the real trouble starts when you ignore the past. It can be challenging to understand how the past affects you and precisely which actions or habits it can cause that don't serve you well now. Changing things means consciously revealing all the parts of your past, understanding and examining them, and attempting to resolve leftover internal and external issues. Despite this not being an easy process, it's a simple one, and it's critical to stop being controlled by the past in ways you may not yet fully understand.

In this chapter, I address how your past could affect you, discuss the many available gifts from clearing up blocks, and give you tangible tools to overcome any impediments you find along your path.

The Gift of Uncovering Your Past

Identifying the impact of your past is an essential part of your life journey. But the good news is that there are so many benefits you have yet to realize. Here are some of the most essential gifts you'll experience from healing your past:

More Space for Good Things

Discarding emotional garbage creates space for new, healthy beliefs and values. Identifying messages that hold you back and restrict you allows you to eliminate negative mental messaging that prevents you from being who you were created to be. Replace the dark with the bright.

New Thoughts, Better You

This process unveils a new and better version of yourself, with fewer feelings of fear, anxiety, stress, and remorse. You'll find yourself more serene, cheerful, patient, and tolerant. Change what you focus on, alter the messages you tell yourself, and you can create a new truth. When you free yourself from negative messaging, you create a new positive outlook on who you are. Then, you can begin to see yourself as successful, talented, and worthwhile. Which you are. And, most importantly, what you see in yourself is what you will become.

Improved Relationships

Freedom from the past improves relationships with your spouse, children, friends, colleagues, and coworkers. You will see them improve as you enjoy your new outlook on the world. It is not simply magical but happens because you will stop projecting your negative feelings or fears onto others. You will no longer feel threatened, frightened, or insecure. You begin to believe in yourself, seeing the best in those around you. Integrity, accountability, and empathy will be the foundations of your relationships. You won't take emotional hostages, and others will no longer have control over your happiness.

Inspiring Others

You won't realize it initially, but your journey will inspire others. Acquaintances around you will witness your progress in overcoming the hurdles in your past and growing to a new reality. They will see your growth and appreciate your more positive outlook. And they will want the same gifts for themselves. Your growth and change will show others they are capable of this, too.

Freedom

Most importantly, getting rid of barriers of the past will help you begin to experience true personal freedom. Old messaging, other's opinions of you, and circumstances in your world used to trap you, but not anymore. Old shame, remorse, resentment, and regret will no longer control your happiness. You will become more independent, having the confidence to chart your path. You will no longer be limited by what others say or think about you. You will fully realize that your success is not dependent on any other person. And you will see that you have the tools and skills to accomplish your goals. Who doesn't want that?

Hurdles of the Past

Negative Messaging

So often, as you grow up, you're told negative things by your parents, family, or friends. Even if they are said in jest, the result is that they can limit your future. Whether or not what was said is true, it suddenly becomes part of your reality. Some of these messages made you feel unworthy or without value. They may have said, "You don't work hard enough," or "You've always been sloppy." "You have toxic relationships," "You're lazy," "You aren't too bright," or "You'll have a tough time getting ahead in life." Hearing these cause them to become part of you. Sometimes, those experiences still affect us today, such as being cut from a team or mistreated in a traumatic relationship. They can control you, maybe even without knowing. To get free, your task is to uncover them and resolve them.

Past Deeds – Shame and Guilt
Perhaps there was a time that you wronged someone and still feel remorse. If you have not cleaned the wrong up or made it right, it can plague you, secretly gnawing at you and affecting your actions and relationships.

Resentments
Have you ever felt angry at someone for something they did to you and felt powerless to stop or change it? And that feeling keeps coming back and festering? Resentment is one of the most insidious and harmful negative emotions you feel. But many, even most of us, experience them, and often without knowing or understanding them.

Regret
Have you ever said something that you wish you hadn't? And every day, even now, it bothers you that you said it. Or, have you ever made a decision not to pursue something and then profoundly regretted that you did not give it an opportunity? Regret is a powerful emotion that, if not resolved, can destroy happiness and limit our success.

Getting Started
Now that you see the benefits of uncovering past events, you may

wonder how you will get there. First, start by understanding that discovering pieces of your past and how it has affected you will take a lot of work and courage. Accept that the process will take some time. Let's get into the exact steps of the method with a proven success track record.

How to Uncover Your Past

1. Begin by finding a quiet place to be alone and uninterrupted.

2. Remove all possible distractions. (Turn that phone to airplane mode)

3. Have a pad of paper or a laptop nearby to make notes (turn off your message and email notifications).

4. Now, systematically review each stage of your life and see what memories and emotional feelings come up for each one.

What to Ask Yourself:

Reflect on past stories you were told about yourself, your characteristics, life, and surrounding circumstances. Consider what was said about you.

Ask yourself these questions to help you to identify messages:

- What were you raised to believe?

- What did your parents tell you life is all about?

- What did your friends and family tell about you, who you are, your capabilities, and your limitations?

- What family sayings and mottos do you still think about today?

- What did your friends teach you, and what messages did you receive from them?

- Have you had any traumatic events, and how did they make

you feel?

- When you think about your youth, is there anything that makes you uncomfortable, hurt, or sad?

Shame and Guilt

Sometimes, you feel guilty about something in your past that still eats at you.

Ask yourself these questions to help you identify shame or guilt:

- Have you harmed any person or institution?

- Have you done something you're ashamed of?

- Is there something in your past you wish you had handled differently?

- Is there anyone whom you wronged that you haven't reconciled?

Resentments

The dictionary defines resentment as a "bitter indignation at having been treated unfairly." Some have called it "victim anger." Resentment is an adverse emotional reaction to being mistreated. It often involves an underlying sense of being wronged by another person without justification. Reflect on anyone against you who has any resentments. Make a list of each person or circumstance you resent.

Ask yourself these questions to help you to identify resentments:

- Is there anyone who wronged you?

- Do you have any resentments today?

- What part of your core was affected by their actions?

- How did that make you feel?

- Did you play any part in the events that led to that resentment?

- Have you ever addressed that grievance with that person?

Regret

Think about actions you wish you would have taken differently. Write them down.

Ask yourself these questions to help you to identify regrets:

- Is there anything you did in your life you wish you hadn't?

- Or some choice you turned down and wished you had made a different choice?

- Do you contemplate any of those today?

- Do they still bother you?

Getting a Clean Slate

How do you free yourself from those experiences that still influence you today? Let's address each area.

Past Messages

Now that you have identified your thoughts, acknowledge that many of your past messages are only sometimes accurate, and most prove unhelpful. Do those stories you were told in your past by friends and family help you? If they don't support your current journey, throw them out and remove those thoughts from your mind.   Choose to be no longer influenced by these harmful ideas. *Remember:* just because someone said them to you does not mean they are real. They do not have to define you. Eliminate them from your conscious thoughts.

Shame and Guilt

Are there things you did in your past that you still need to rectify? Do these come into your mind repeatedly, maybe even daily? Is there anyone you hurt or harmed in your past that you still need to apologize to? Is there someone who believes you're responsible for their pain that you have not reconciled with?

Secret wrongs will often continue to trouble a person. However, the relief from making things right and forgiveness can heal you, even if just from yourself. It's time to clear up your side of the street. Doing so will free you from that gnawing feeling eating away at you. Free yourself from the remorse that you carry with you.

If you identify a past action or lack of that that still bothers you today, find a way to make amends with the person involved. Let them know what you did, that you were wrong, and want to make it right (whatever it takes). A little scary? Yes. But so worth it. You will feel genuinely free after you have made amends for any of those events.

Resentments

Sometimes, an event from the past can cause negative feelings of ill will toward someone or something. You can keep re-experiencing injustices, whether real or perceived, and anger flows toward a person, institution, or situation. Resentment is persistence in holding onto that anger. Struggling to release resentments happens when remembering the wrongs, and you feel like a victim again long after the original injury.

Many lawyers experience resentment over such things as partners who treat them abusively, clients who file malpractice claims against them without a basis, other attorneys who engage in nasty conduct or make groundless claims, and support staff who regularly drop the ball on their assignments. Has that happened to you?

The pain eats away at you inside when you hold onto those feelings toward someone else who wrongly harmed you.

There is truth in the phrase, "Feeling resentful about someone else is like you drinking poison but waiting for the other person to die." When you feel resentful, the responsible party is often unaware, may not care, and is not affected. So, the only person you're harming is yourself by allowing the person who wronged you to be in control of your happiness.

Resentment can even become obsessive, and you may feel unable to stop reliving the pain. The good news is that you can overcome our feelings of resentment.

How Do You Free Yourself From Resentment?

Despite how it sometimes feels, you control your attitudes and thoughts. You can free yourself from the pain of festering over resentments. Here are seven tips you can use to overcome that continual anger you feel about something that happened to you:

Understand and Acknowledge Your Emotions

Reflect on what happened to understand your feelings about it. Ask: Why are you feeling the way you do? How did what happened harm you? How were you affected? Allow yourself to feel those feelings. Understanding what happened and how you think is the first and crucial step. It's healthy to admit, "I have a resentment."

Accepting Your Role

Is there anything that you did to cause or contribute to it? Almost always, some action or behavior on our part is related to what happened. Take responsibility for our piece of the event. Accepting our role is not only an action of personal responsibility but a step towards freeing ourselves from the victim mentality at the heart of our resentment.

Sharing Your Feelings

Reach out to a trusted family member or friend, and tell them what happened and how you feel. It can be cathartic to stop holding those feelings inside and start voicing them with someone you trust. You may also see the situation differently or obtain new insight into what happened and why.

Take Action Where You Can

You have the power to choose to take action about what happened. Is there anything you can do about it? Journal about it? Speak directly to the person? Write a letter? There's no correct answer. But reflect on whether there's something constructive you can do, and then do it.

Practice Acceptance

You cannot change the person. You cannot undo what happened. It is what it is. So, accept it. Stop resisting it. Stop arguing about it in your mind and continuing to feel angry. Accept it as being what happened and that you cannot change it. That will help us to move past it.

Forgive

Isn't it hard to forgive someone who harmed us without reason? Of course. But It's a step toward creating our freedom. When you feel angry over what someone did to you, you only hurt yourself, not the wrongdoer. Forgiveness doesn't justify what happened and is not an admission that what happened was not wrong. It does, though, stop that other person from continuing to cause us pain. It frees us from the self-inflicted anger you continue to feel. Forgiveness is self-empowering. It ends the other person's control over our happiness.

Be Grateful

Instead of stewing on some past wrong, what do you have to be thankful for today? Write a list of all the blessings in your life and reflect on them. You feel serene and at peace when you focus on what you can be grateful for.

Regret

Regret is powerful. A negative emotion occurs when you believe your past actions would have led to a better outcome if changed. It's often associated with feelings of guilt and shame. You may blame yourself because the alternative decision would have been much better. Regret is often a long-lasting negative emotion that you cannot eliminate. It's a genuine reaction to a disappointing event, a choice you wish you could undo, something you said you wanted to take back. It's a heavy, intrusive, burdensome emotion that sometimes takes too long to get rid of.

How Does Regret Affect You?

Handling regret is much more complicated because of the negative emotions connected to it – shame, guilt, sorrow, and helplessness. When you struggle with regret, you beat yourself for past choices or actions. It's exhausting, draining joy and fulfillment out of your life. You can get stuck, looking back, unable to move forward. It can cause chronic stress and anxiety by constantly reliving what you could have done differently.

How To Free Yourself From Regret

The good news is that while regret is powerful, you can manage it. Here are the steps:

Acknowledge Your Feelings

Reflect on why you feel bad. What is the cause of your negative emotions? Being aware of it helps you to know how to manage it. It never works to deny or squash the feeling of regret.

Forgive Yourself

It's time to stop beating yourself up. You are human, not perfect. You cannot change the choices you make or the actions you take. There's no benefit to continuing to live in self-blame. You easily forgive others; why not yourself? Permit yourself to get it wrong sometimes.

Use It As a Learning Opportunity

Objectively evaluate what happened. What could you have done differently? How can I change my thinking or behavior to achieve a better result next time?

Conclusion

Our past contains harmful messages and negative feelings – resentment, disappointment, shame, and remorse. By examining our past, you can discover those hurdles that affect us today. Applying these steps, you can free yourself to live fully and happily. You deserve that.

Prison 2:
Overthinking The Future

(The Cost of Overthinking: Why It's Time to Stop Worrying About the Future)

"If you want to conquer overthinking, bring your mind to the present moment and reconnect it with the immediate world."
– Amit Ray

Do you think about the future and wonder how something will work out?

Questions like:

Will I win this case?
Will I make partner?
Will that new client hire me?
Will my children get into the colleges they dream of?

Lawyers commonly spend much of their valuable time planning for the future, analyzing options, and strategizing the best courses of action. But that can turn into overthinking and cause unnecessary stress and anxiety. You can get stuck in the future. It happens to many, and I know it does to me.

Overthinking can also lead to indecisiveness and a lack of productivity, making it difficult to take action toward achieving the goals you're spending so much time planning. You can stop worrying, and you're about to get some tools and strategies to help you manage your thoughts and return your focus to the present moment. You will explore the problems with overthinking the future and provide practical tips to help you stop overthinking and live more mindfully.

What's The Problem With Living In The Future?

The most significant impact is on how you feel. It's great to have dreams, hopes, and visions and to plan for the future. But, are you living too much in the future? You can create an emotional nightmare if you focus too much on the future and the unknown.

Overthinking the future can significantly impact your mental health. Constantly worrying about what may or may not happen in the future can lead to anxiety, stress, and overwhelming feelings. This can cause your thoughts to spiral out of control, making it difficult to focus on the present moment or take action toward achieving your goals. Overthinking can also lead to negative self-talk and self-doubt, damaging your self-esteem and confidence. And in extreme cases, overthinking can contribute to developing anxiety disorders or depression. Therefore, finding healthy ways to manage our thoughts and emotions and bring our focus back to the present moment is essential.

What happens often is you're living in fear of what might happen. You are afraid of something that has not happened yet. You begin suffering the pain now of what is only a future possibility. If it happens, you suffer that pain twice, now and when it happens. If it doesn't, you suffer that pain for nothing. When you live in the future, you allow a merely possible future event to ruin today's happiness.

Issues With Living In the Future

But there are other negative impacts as well. These are some other problems you encounter when you spend too much time living in the future:

You Won't Enjoy the Present

There's so much happiness and beauty in our present life, but you sometimes miss today's gifts if you focus on tomorrow. You may find it difficult to enjoy and appreciate the present moment fully. I know I am often someplace wholly incredible with people I know and care about, but my mind wanders to someplace else where I will be later. I rob myself of the joy of the present.

Missed Opportunities

Focusing solely on the future can cause us to miss out on options available in the present.

It Affects Our Relationships

Worrying about what our friends, family, and spouse will do, how they will behave, and what will happen can create negative stress in otherwise healthy relationships.

It Can Create Adverse Outcomes

Worrying about the future and projecting ahead to a negative result can be a self-fulfilling prophecy. If you focus on too many negative thoughts about what will happen, the results are often less successful than they otherwise would be.

Loss of Spontaneity

Constantly thinking about the future can lead to a loss of spontaneity and a lack of ability to enjoy impromptu experiences.

You have no control over the future. It only creates frustration when trying to control something you cannot. Your story still stands to be written, and trying to control it creates frustration and disappointment. The future is not a healthy place to live, don't you agree?

How To Stop Overthinking The Future

Are you tired of experiencing that anxiety and stress? Finally, you can break out of the prison of the future. Here are eight tools:

Mindfulness

Be engaged in the moment. You can focus on the present instead of worrying about the future. Be aware of your thoughts and feelings. Are you living in the present or obsessing about the future?

Redirect Your Thoughts

When you're stuck worrying about the future or are anxious about something that has not happened, choose a different idea. Redirect yourself to the present. Choose to see a positive outcome instead of a negative one. When mindful that our mind is stuck in the future, we can return to the present.

Journaling

Writing down your thoughts and feelings can help you process them and gain a new perspective. You can use a journal to record your worries and fears and explore ways to address them.

Breathing Exercises

Deep breathing exercises can help you relax and reduce anxiety. Try inhaling deeply for four seconds, holding your breath for four seconds, and exhaling for four seconds. Repeat this cycle several times.

Gratitude

Focusing on what you're grateful for can help shift your focus away from worrying about the future. Start a gratitude journal or take a few minutes each day to reflect on what you're grateful for.

Visualization

Imagine positive outcomes and reduce anxiety about the future. Visualize yourself successfully dealing with challenges or achieving your goals. Choose to see your success instead of visualizing the worst result.

Get Into Action

When I am stuck in the future, thinking about what I will be doing tomorrow, I return to the present and purposefully engage in what is in front of me. If you paralyze yourself worrying about the future, start a purposeful activity. Get started on doing what helps bring you success – call that prospective client, prepare your case, etc. Getting into action helps to destroy the paralysis of overthinking the future.

Seek Support

Find a friend or trusted adviser to talk to. Open yourself to someone you trust. Obtain encouragement from those who care about you. Use the wise counsel of an experienced mentor who can guide your thinking and help you to refocus.

Conclusion

As lawyers, responsible planning and worrying about the future obsessively happens naturally. But living in the future can negatively affect your mental health and prevent you from living in the present and working toward your goals. By practicing mindfulness, journaling, breathing exercises, gratitude, visualization, and obtaining support, you can learn to manage your thoughts and emotions and bring your focus back to the present.

Remember that it's okay to plan for the future, but it's essential not to let your worries and fears consume you. By using these tools and strategies, you can break free from the cycle of overthinking and start living a more fulfilling and mindful life. So take a deep breath, let go of your worries, and focus on the now. The future will take care of itself.

Prison 3: Self-Doubt and Imposter Syndrome

(The Hidden Doubts: Unmasking Imposter Syndrome in the Legal Profession)

"Never, ever, ever, write off anything you've achieved as merely being lucky. You're not lucky: you're hard-working and capable. Don't ever question it."
– Charlene Walters

Have you ever felt that you were not as good as other people think you are?

Have you ever doubted your ability to achieve what you already have?

Do you see yourself as unworthy or not good at what you do, even though others think you are?

Have you ever felt you didn't belong?

Or even, "What am I doing here?"

I know I have struggled with some of those thoughts. This self-doubt is often labeled as "imposter syndrome." But trust me, if you have ever felt that way, you're not alone.

Imposter syndrome, an all-too-common phenomenon experienced by professionals in various fields, can be particularly pervasive among lawyers. Despite our impressive qualifications and extensive legal knowledge, training, and success, many of us are plagued by self-doubt, fearing that we do not truly deserve our accomplishments or that others will consider our expertise inadequate.

However, imposter syndrome is a psychological barrier that can hinder our professional growth and diminish our confidence. In this chapter, you'll delve into the intricacies of imposter syndrome within the legal profession and provide practical strategies to help lawyers overcome this debilitating mindset, empowering them to embrace their true capabilities and thrive in their careers.

What's Imposter Syndrome?

Imposter syndrome is a psychological phenomenon in which legal professionals experience persistent self-doubt and inadequacy despite their accomplishments, qualifications, and expertise. Lawyers grappling with imposter syndrome often fear being exposed as frauds or feeling unworthy of their professional success.

They may attribute their achievements to luck or external factors rather than recognizing their skills and competence. Imposter syndrome can manifest as a barrier to career advancement, causing lawyers to undermine their abilities, second-guess their decisions, and constantly need to prove themselves, ultimately impacting their confidence and overall well-being. Have you ever felt that?

Imposter syndrome involves feelings of self-doubt that exist despite significant experience and accomplishments. It's much more common than anyone thinks. Those imposter feelings are the conflict between how you see yourself and how others perceive you. When others praise you, you still do not see yourself as successful, but perhaps just lucky or the benefit of good timing.

The imposter feelings reflect the doubt about your talents and abilities that do not align with how others see you. You respond to those feelings by working ever harder, trying to prove yourself, to make yourself feel worthy. The cycle continues. You accept successes as given but beat yourself up about any mistakes or failures. Not handled, this cycle can lead to guilt and even depression.

Does Imposter Syndrome Exist?

Sadly, many high-performing, successful attorneys have struggled with imposter syndrome. Unfortunately, it afflicts some of the best and brightest. It seems irrational from the outside, but It's real.

I was striving to be as good as possible at a very early age. I did exceptionally well in school. I was at the top of my high school, college, and law school classes. I clerked in federal court for one of the best judges on the bench. I learned to try cases at a boutique litigation firm. I was a very successful trial attorney. I did well in court. I managed my law firm. Yet, somehow, it seemed like a mirage, not real. I had thoughts that I was not capable and that I was not good at what I did. Others perceived me as top-notch, yet I questioned my validity as a trial attorney and a manager. How could that be?

Why Do You Experience Imposter Syndrome?

So, where does this imposter syndrome come from? Why do you suffer from it? It's not clear why some of us are afflicted with it; it may be from a sense of perfectionism or experiences from childhood.

Our profession can contribute to feelings of inadequacy. High standards, intense competition, and constant scrutiny create an environment for self-comparison and self-doubt. The legal field often emphasizes perfectionism, leaving little room for mistakes or vulnerability. Lawyers may fear falling short of these rigid expectations, leading to a sense of being an imposter.

Furthermore, the culture within our profession itself can perpetuate the imposter syndrome. The competitive nature of the field, coupled with a lack of open discussion about self-doubt and vulnerability, can create an atmosphere where lawyers feel isolated in their experiences. You feel alone, as if no one else thinks like you do. The fear of appearing weak or incapable may prevent us from seeking support or acknowledging our struggles, exacerbating imposter syndrome.

How Does Imposter Syndrome Affect You?

Imposter syndrome profoundly impacts everyone. It erodes self-confidence, making you doubt your abilities and expertise. Maybe you constantly question your competence, leading to heightened anxiety and stress. Imposter syndrome can also hinder career advancement; some may hesitate to take on new challenges or opportunities for fear of being considered inadequate. As a result, you may miss chances for growth and development.

Additionally, imposter syndrome can strain relationships with colleagues and clients, as lawyers may struggle to project confidence and assertiveness. The constant need to prove oneself can lead to burnout and a lack of work-life balance. Overall, imposter syndrome undermines a lawyer's self-worth and hampers their ability to thrive professionally.

In short, it creates uncertainty and doubt. It affects our happiness, our confidence, and our success. It can create stress and anxiety. You are afraid to take action. You constantly doubt yourself. Worry and fear consume us. You are unhappy and unfulfilled.

How Do You Overcome Imposter Syndrome?

The good news: It's manageable. You can eliminate its power. You can use several tools to overcome imposter syndrome and regain confidence in your professional abilities. Here's how:

Self-Reflection and Awareness

Take the time to reflect on your achievements, skills, and strengths. Be aware of your thoughts. Recognize that imposter syndrome is a common experience and that your feelings of doubt are not necessarily grounded in reality.

Seek Support and Mentorship

Reach out to trusted mentors, colleagues, or professional support networks. Share your concerns and self-doubt with individuals who can provide guidance, reassurance, and perspective. Engaging in open conversations about imposter syndrome can help normalize the experience and provide valuable insights. Share your feelings with others you trust on a confidential basis. You'll find other people have the same experiences. Giving voice to your feelings reduces their power over you. Others can also give you a reality check and help you see your talent.

Keep a Success Journal

Create a journal to record your achievements, big or small. Documenting positive feedback, successful cases, or instances where you made a difference can remind you of your capabilities during moments of self-doubt.

Focus on Facts, Not Feelings

What's your track record? What have you accomplished? When you analyze your history, you'll see that the facts do not support your imposter feelings. Instead, look for the evidence that counters those feelings.

Embrace Constructive Feedback

Instead of viewing feedback as a confirmation of your inadequacy, see it as an opportunity for growth and improvement. Recognize that feedback is a normal part of professional development and doesn't diminish your expertise.

Strive For Excellence, Not Perfection

Understand that perfection is an unrealistic standard. Embrace the idea that mistakes and setbacks are opportunities for learning and growth. Adopt a mindset of continuous improvement rather than striving for unattainable perfection. You will never be perfect, but you can succeed at being excellent. When seeking perfection, you fail, supporting your feelings of being an imposter. Make excellence your goal.

Stop Comparing Yourself

Whenever you compare, you constantly come up short. You are all different. You all have other talents and skills. Instead, focus on your successes and achievements.

Accept Your Mistakes

'Learn from them. In each failure, there's a lesson that helps us grow and become better. That setback is an opportunity for growth, not a definition of who you are.

Change Your Script

Accept yourself as you are. Believe in the gifts that you have. Affirm what you have accomplished and what you're capable of. Create a vision of success. Discard the feelings of doubt and self-criticism. Challenge negative self-talk and replace it with positive affirmations. Be kind to yourself. You can change the story you tell yourself and truly change our lives.

Focus on Helping Others

Shifting your focus from self-doubt to assisting others can be empowering. Use your legal expertise to support and advocate for clients, pro bono work, or community initiatives. Making a positive impact can reaffirm your value and purpose as a lawyer.

Conclusion

For a long time, I struggled with imposter syndrome. I now know what I am good at, how to serve others, and how to succeed. I also know the areas where I can grow, change and improve. I know I could be better. But I also understand my gifts and how I can be helpful to others. You, too, can overcome any imposter feelings.

Overcoming imposter syndrome is not an overnight process. Still, with persistence, self-reflection, and implementing practical strategies, you can break free from self-doubt and reclaim your confidence. Remember, you're not alone in experiencing imposter syndrome; It's a shared struggle among many accomplished legal professionals.

By acknowledging your accomplishments, embracing your expertise, seeking support from mentors and colleagues, and reframing your mindset, you can navigate the challenges of imposter syndrome and emerge as a more decisive, more self-assured lawyer. Let go of self-limiting beliefs, celebrate your achievements, and embark on a journey of self-empowerment that will enable you to reach new heights in your legal career. You're deserving, capable, and destined for greatness – believe in yourself, for you're an exceptional lawyer!

Prison 4: Burnout

*"Give up the delusion that burnout is the inevitable
cost of success."*
–Arianna Huffington

Have you ever felt overwhelmed at work?

That you simply cannot handle anymore?

**Although you loved your profession, are you tired of
it and getting frustrated now?**

Have you ever felt burned out?

Burnout is common. So many lawyers are overwhelmed, overworked, stressed out, and unhappy. How can you change this?

In the fast-paced world of law, the demands on us are high, and the pressures are constant. The specter of burnout looms large, casting its shadow over even the most passionate and dedicated attorneys. As you navigate complex cases, tight deadlines, and the intricate dance of client expectations, the toll on your mental and physical well-being can become overwhelming.

This chapter unravels the threads of burnout that often entangle lawyers. More importantly, you illuminate the path towards recovery and resilience. You will look deeply into the intricacies of lawyer burnout, dissect its causes, and lay bare its effects. More importantly, actionable steps and strategies will help you manage burnout and thrive in the demanding landscape of the legal profession. It's time to rewrite the narrative, transforming burnout from an inevitable consequence to a conquerable challenge.

What Causes Burnout?

Several significant factors converge in our practice to sow the seeds of burnout among lawyers. These factors intertwine and amplify each other, creating a perfect storm that can erode the well-being of even the most dedicated lawyers.

One of the primary culprits is the unrelenting workload that lawyers often face. The ceaseless stream of cases and demanding deadlines leave minimal room for respite. This unyielding pressure is further exacerbated by the high-stakes nature of the matters you handle, where the outcome of a case can profoundly impact our clients' lives.

The inherently adversarial nature of the legal system can also lead to emotionally taxing interactions, further draining our emotional resources of lawyers. You are always living in conflict. Moreover, the relentless pursuit of billable hours to meet financial targets can eclipse the importance of self-care, pushing us to our limits.

Our self-worth is defined by what we do professionally. Our professional success validates our self-worth. How often have you been accustomed to saying, "What do you do?" You constantly evaluate yourself as proficient based on your success. You increasingly take on more because It's a badge of success.

Moreover, our financial security is directly related to how you do professionally. If you want to achieve your monetary goals, you must be successful in your career. As a result, you feel pressured to work harder, more hours, and more intensely to solidify your financial future.

In addition, you're committed to helping our clients. You are problem solvers. You want to serve others. So, our client needs our help. You often want to dive in and help, no matter the time of day or hours required. You tell yourself that the cost doesn't matter because It's what you do to help our clients. You justify this to our family and friends by offering excellent service to those in need.

Then, of course, the boss keeps giving us more and more work despite an already full plate. Paying no heed to our demands, the partner may pile more assignments on us even though you're already overwhelmed by too much work. Work interferes with our personal or family commitments. These factors combine to create a perfect storm of possible burnout.

What Are The Warning Signs Of Burnout?

Recognizing the warning signs and symptoms of burnout is crucial for taking proactive steps toward managing our well-being. Here are some common indicators that you might be experiencing burnout:

Persistent Exhaustion
You feel chronically tired, both physically and emotionally, regardless of the amount of rest or sleep.

Decreased Performance
Noticing a decline in the quality of work, reduced efficiency, or difficulty concentrating on tasks.

Cynicism and Detachment
Developing a cynical or negative attitude towards work, clients, or attorneys. Feeling emotionally detached from cases or clients.

Reduced Motivation
Losing interest or passion for work that was once engaging and fulfilling. Finding it challenging to muster enthusiasm for tasks.

Emotional Rollercoaster
You are experiencing frequent mood swings, irritability, or emotional instability that disrupts professional interactions.

Physical Symptoms

Suffering from frequent headaches, stomach issues, or other physical symptoms often associated with stress.

Isolation

Withdrawing from social interactions, avoiding colleagues, or isolating oneself from professional networks.

Insomnia or Sleep Disturbances

Struggling to fall asleep, stay asleep, or wake up feeling unrefreshed despite adequate time in bed.

Lack of Self-Care

Ignoring personal well-being by neglecting exercise, hobbies, and activities that used to bring joy.

Increased Substance Use

Relying on alcohol, caffeine, or other substances to cope with stress or fatigue.

Forgetfulness

Experiencing memory lapses, forgetfulness, or difficulty concentrating on tasks.

Impaired Decision-Making

Making impulsive or careless decisions due to mental fatigue or overwhelm.

Lack of Satisfaction

Feeling unfulfilled even after achieving professional milestones or successes.

Work-Life Imbalance

Struggling to maintain a healthy separation between work and personal life, with work consistently encroaching on personal time.

Recognizing these signs early on can help us proactively address burnout and prevent its escalation.

What Are The Consequences Of Burnout For Lawyers?

Left uncorrected, these behaviors can lead to severe consequences. The implications can be dire when not heeding those symptoms and taking proactive steps to prevent burnout.

You can suffer physically. Prolonged burnout leads to various physical health issues, including chronic fatigue, headaches, digestive problems, and compromised immune function. You're also at a higher risk of developing mental health challenges such as anxiety disorders, depression, and even substance abuse as a coping mechanism.

Equally important, you can suffer professionally. Burnout can erode the quality of your work, leading to decreased attention to detail, impaired decision-making, and reduced productivity. It can damage your professional reputation. The emotional detachment often accompanies burnout can negatively affect lawyer-client relationships, leading to decreased empathy and communication breakdowns.

You may encounter workplace conflicts due to increased irritability, decreased tolerance for stress, and strained interactions with attorneys and partners. You may become less enthusiastic and satisfied, potentially driving you to contemplate leaving the profession altogether. Burnout may hinder your career advancement, limit opportunities for growth, and prevent you from reaching your full potential.

It affects your life as a whole. Burnout can intensify the divide between work and personal life, causing relationships, hobbies, and self-care to take a back seat. The emotional toll of burnout can permeate into all areas of life, leading to a diminished overall quality of life and reduced enjoyment of daily activities.

Preventing burnout can safeguard your mental, emotional, and physical health while ensuring your effectiveness as advocates.

Twelve Tips for Preventing Burnout

The good news is you can restore a balance. Mitigating burnout requires a multifaceted approach that combines self-awareness, proactive strategies, and a commitment to holistic well-being. Here are essential steps lawyers can follow to prevent or manage burnout: You can do a great job at work, have a wonderful home life, and feel fulfilled. Here is how::

Communicate

Discuss your workload and stressors with supervisors or mentors. They may offer guidance, suggest resources, or help adjust your responsibilities. Let your business associates and your family know what time you have, your ability to work, and your needs. Sometimes, we hide our time limitations and frustrations, creating more stress. It can be freeing not to keep our work frustrations secret. Sharing them with our spouse, close friend, or trusted coworker can help us receive support and understanding.

Breaks

Incorporate regular short breaks throughout the day to recharge. Stepping away from your desk and engaging in quick relaxation activities can improve productivity. Go outside, walk, or do something that clears your mind and recharges your batteries. It's essential every day to disconnect, get some fresh air, and get some brief time away from the stresses at work.

Say No

Evaluate your commitments and learn to decline additional tasks when your plate is already full. Saying no assertively is a crucial skill to prevent overwhelm. Just say no when it's too much and you cannot do it. You often say yes to something you cannot do and then get frustrated at the person who asked you. It's hard. You want to please our boss or satisfy our client's needs. But sometimes, you simply cannot and must learn to say "no" properly and respectfully. Look for alternatives. Perhaps find others who can help, navigate to a different time frame, or seek other options for getting it done.

Set Boundaries

Establish clear boundaries between work and personal life. Avoid checking emails or working during off-hours to create a space for rest and rejuvenation. Give them your undivided attention when you're with your family or loved ones.

Prioritize and Monitor Workload

Set priorities at work. First things first, always. Plan what you need to do and when you need to do it. Keep track of your workload and recognize when it becomes unmanageable. Reach out for assistance or reevaluate priorities when necessary.

Organize Your Schedule

Plan your day. Schedule your work time, your breaks, and your family time. Make a list of what you're going to do and when. It helps. And, when you create your schedule, try to stick to it. Implement effective time management strategies to stay focused during work hours and make time for breaks.

Take Time Off

Go somewhere you love. Find time to get a break from the demands of your job. You deserve and need the time off. Disconnect from the office.

Unplug

Take intentional breaks from technology and screens to reduce digital fatigue and promote mental relaxation. When you're at home, you can unplug from work. Do not check your emails. It can wait until tomorrow. You do not need to connect to work 24/7.

Self-Care

Make self-care a non-negotiable priority. Engage in activities that bring joy, exercise regularly, eat nourishing foods, and ensure you're getting enough sleep. Dedicate time to hobbies or interests outside of work to rejuvenate your mind and find fulfillment beyond the legal sphere. Engage in regular physical activity, as it can reduce stress, boost mood, and increase overall well-being. You must take care of yourself so you have the energy and strength to perform at work and to be present at home.

Obtain Support

Consult a professional mentor to help you find clarity, confidence, and contentment. Maintain a supportive network of colleagues, friends, and family members who can provide emotional support and a sounding board for challenges. Consider seeking professional therapy or counseling to explore stress management techniques and address underlying issues.

Celebrate Achievements

You've all had victories but take them for granted too often. Acknowledge your successes, no matter how small. Celebrating achievements can boost motivation and help counteract feelings of burnout.

Reflect and Reevaluate

Periodically assess your career goals, values, and overall job satisfaction. Is this the place for you? Are you doing what you want to do? Is your career aligned with your values? Make adjustments if your current path is contributing to burnout.

Conclusion

You encounter so many professional stresses. Our drive to succeed, demanding partners and clients, and overwhelming workloads combine to make us work harder and harder and harder. You work almost around the clock without boundaries. You suffer physically and emotionally. 'You are frustrated and stressed, our relationships struggle, and the quality of our work declines. You do not have to be unfulfilled and burned out.

By communicating our needs, taking breaks, learning to say no, prioritizing and organizing, taking time off, unplugging, and taking care of yourself, you can enjoy success and freedom in ways you always dreamed of. By acknowledging the signs, embracing self-care, and implementing the strategies shared here, you possess the tools to transform burnout from an adversary into a challenge you can triumph over. Remember that your worth transcends billable hours, your impact reaches beyond courtrooms, and your well-being is paramount. Your journey toward a healthier, more balanced legal practice begins now – a journey that promises not only to redefine the way you approach your work but also to reshape the legal profession for the better.

Prison 5: Perfectionism

(Escaping the Perfectionism Trap: A Guide for Lawyers to Achieve Balance and Success)

"Perfectionism is not a quest for the best. It's a pursuit of the worst in ourselves, the part that tells us that nothing we do will ever be good enough — that we should try again."
–Julia Cameron

Are you often never delighted with your work?

Are you afraid to release that pleading or memo until you check it repeatedly?

Are you too critical of yourself?

As lawyers, pursuing excellence and attention to detail is a fundamental part of our profession. However, when these tendencies become excessive and unrealistic, they can lead to perfectionism and hurt our well-being and professional success. Perfectionistic lawyers may feel constant pressure to meet unrealistic expectations, leading to high stress levels, anxiety, and burnout. They may struggle to delegate tasks, spend too much time on minor details, and fear failure. Sound familiar? This chapter analyzes the consequences of perfectionism in the legal profession and provides practical tools for overcoming it, promoting a healthier work-life balance and overall well-being.

What Is Perfectionism In Lawyers?

Perfectionism for lawyers is the tendency to set extremely high standards for oneself and others in the legal profession and to be overly critical of one's work and the work of others. You feel a strong drive to achieve perfection in every aspect of our legal practice, often at the expense of personal well-being and work-life balance.

Perfectionistic lawyers may feel constant pressure to meet unrealistic expectations, leading to high stress levels, anxiety, and burnout. They may also need help delegating tasks to others, as they feel that only they can do the work to their desired level of quality.

While striving for excellence is admirable, excessive perfectionism can harm the legal profession. It can lead to missed deadlines, strained relationships with colleagues, and a focus on minor details rather than the big picture. Lawyers must balance pursuing excellence and caring for their mental and physical health.

Several signs may indicate perfectionism in lawyers. These include:

Setting Unrealistic Expectations

You may set high standards that are nearly impossible to achieve, leading to a constant feeling of dissatisfaction and failure.

Being Overly Critical

Perfectionistic lawyers may be excessively self-critical and critical of others, focusing on minor mistakes rather than the overall outcome.

Difficulty Delegating Tasks

A perfectionistic lawyer may feel he's the only one who can do the job properly and has difficulty delegating tasks to others.

Spending Too Much Time on Tasks

Perfectionistic lawyers may spend excessive time on tasks, even if they're not necessary or efficient because they want everything to be perfect.

Fear of Failure

Perfectionistic lawyers may intensely fear failure and avoid taking risks or pursuing opportunities that could potentially fail.

Struggle with Work-Life Balance

Perfectionistic lawyers may prioritize work over personal life and find it difficult to relax or take breaks.

If you or someone you know displays these signs, seeking extra support and help to find a healthy balance between pursuing excellence and taking care of oneself may be essential.

Why Do So Many Lawyers Struggle With Perfectionism?

Perfectionism in lawyers can have various causes, including:

Personality Traits

Some lawyers may have personality traits that make them more susceptible to perfectionism, such as a strong need for control, a fear of failure, or a tendency towards obsessiveness.

Professional Expectations

Have you ever felt the weight of expectations of yourself and others? The legal profession can emphasize precision and attention to detail, which can contribute to developing perfectionistic tendencies.

Fear of Consequences

Do you ever worry about what will happen if you make a mistake? Lawyers may feel that their work has significant consequences, such as negatively impacting a client's case or reputation, which can increase the pressure to strive for perfection.

High Workload and Pressure

Do you feel pressure from workloads and deadlines? Lawyers often have heavy workloads and face demanding deadlines, creating a sense of urgency to work quickly and perfectly.

Early Life Experiences
Childhood experiences, such as parental pressure to achieve, can contribute to the development of perfectionism in lawyers.

Societal Influences
Does our society honor success? Cultural and societal values that emphasize achievement and success can also contribute to the development of perfectionism in lawyers.

It's essential to recognize the causes of perfectionism to develop strategies to address it and achieve a healthy work-life balance.

How Perfectionism Affects You

Perfectionism harms us in many ways, including:

Burnout
Perfectionistic lawyers may feel constant pressure to meet unrealistic expectations, leading to high stress levels and burnout.

Reduced Productivity
Spending excessive time on tasks and striving for perfection can reduce productivity, as you waste time and energy on minor details rather than the big picture.

Strained Relationships
Being overly critical of oneself and others can lead to strained relationships with colleagues, clients, and others in the legal profession.

Missed Deadlines
Perfectionistic lawyers may struggle to delegate tasks and spend too much time on assignments, leading to missed deadlines and a negative impact on clients.

Health Problems

The stress and pressure associated with perfectionism can lead to physical and mental health problems, such as anxiety, depression, and insomnia.

Reduced Job Satisfaction

Perfectionism can lead to constant dissatisfaction and failure, reducing job satisfaction and overall well-being.

You must recognize the consequences of perfectionism and find ways to manage it effectively, such as setting realistic goals and expectations, delegating tasks, and prioritizing self-care.

How You Can Overcome Perfectionism

There are several tools that lawyers can use, including:

Set Realistic Goals

Often, you have excessively high standards. Setting realistic goals and expectations can reduce the pressure to achieve perfection and promote a healthier work-life balance.

Practice Self-Compassion

Aren't you often too hard on yourself? Being kind to oneself and recognizing that mistakes are a natural part of the learning process can help reduce the fear of failure and promote self-confidence.

Delegate Tasks

You can free yourself by effectively delegating. Learning to delegate tasks to others and trusting that they can do the job properly can help reduce the pressure to do everything oneself.

Prioritize Self-Care

You all know that practicing self-care is so important. Taking care of oneself physically and mentally can help reduce stress and promote overall well-being.

Challenge Negative Self-Talk

Do you find your inner self speaking harshly to yourself? Identifying and challenging negative self-talk, such as "I'm not good enough" or "I must be perfect," can help to reduce the pressure to achieve perfection.

Focus on the Big Picture

What is your primary goal? What are you trying to achieve? Recognizing that perfection is not always necessary or achievable and focusing on the overall outcome rather than minor details can help reduce the pressure to achieve perfection.

Seek Support

Seeking support from colleagues, friends, or mental health professionals can provide a helpful perspective and additional tools for managing perfectionism. An independent mentor can be beneficial in identifying and overcoming a perfectionistic tendency.

Strive for Excellence

Let go of being perfect. Excellence should be our goal.

By utilizing these tools, lawyers can overcome perfectionism and achieve a healthier work-life balance, reducing stress and improving overall well-being.

Conclusion

While pursuing excellence is admirable, excessive perfectionism can harm our well-being and professional success. By recognizing the signs and causes of perfectionism and utilizing tools such as setting realistic goals, practicing self-compassion, delegating tasks, prioritizing self-care, challenging negative self-talk, focusing on the big picture, and seeking support, you can overcome perfectionism and achieve a healthier work-life balance.

Remember that mistakes and imperfections are a natural part of learning and should not define your worth as a lawyer. By embracing a growth mindset and balancing excellence and self-care, you can achieve success and fulfillment in your legal career.

Prison 6: Stress

(Mastering Stress as a Lawyer: Tools and Tips for Success)

"The truth is that stress doesn't come from your boss, your kids, your spouse, traffic jams, health challenges, or other circumstances. It comes from your thoughts about your circumstances."
– Andrew Bernstein

Do you ever feel stressed at work?

Do you often feel overwhelmed by pressure from all sides?

And do you need to figure out how to manage it best so you can enjoy fulfillment in your professional life?

Attorneys face many high-pressure situations and demanding workloads that can lead to stress and burnout. You work long hours in a competitive environment and handle emotionally challenging cases. This constant stress can significantly affect your mental and physical health, job performance, and quality of life. However, you CAN manage that stress and be happy and healthy. Let's explore the primary causes of stress and how that affects you, along with practical tools and techniques that you can use to manage stress and maintain your overall health and happiness.

What Are The Primary Causes Of Our Stress?

You can face pressures from so many different directions. What are they? These are just some:

Billable Hour Requirements

You are always on the clock. You are tracking our time. Measuring our worth in minutes recorded on a timesheet and feeling like we always need more time in the day.

Financial Concerns

If you're a partner in a small firm, you're constantly working on bringing in more work to make enough profits and income. You must generate fees in larger firms to justify our fair share of the revenues. As younger attorneys, you feel compelled to build a book of business to make partners or build leverage. And it always seems that there needs to be more money. After taxes and expenses, there is often not enough money to go around.

Client Pressures

Clients often have high expectations and can be very demanding. It can be challenging to satisfy them. Clients frequently place unreasonable demands on the deadlines and the outcome.

Heavy Workload

You have to manage multiple matters simultaneously, which creates additional pressure.

Other Attorneys

Sadly, one of the worst stresses you face is the conduct of other attorneys. They often engage in unnecessary personal attacks. They may not return calls. They are much more interested in fighting than solving problems.

The Pressure of Failure

In litigation, there are winners and losers. Even the best attorney trying a great case will sometimes lose. That can create real emotional pressures.

High-Stakes Cases

Our cases often have high financial and emotional stakes for our clients, a pressure you carry while you advocate for our clients.

Work-Life Balance

Finding time for family and personal activities, hobbies, and self-care can be difficult when work becomes all-consuming. You can lose sight of what is most important to us. You often work long hours, including weekends and holidays, which can lead to physical and mental exhaustion.

Firm Competiton

In some firms, there's internal competition to do better than the other associates, to bill more hours, and to bring in more clients. Rather than a sense of teamwork, our firm can have stressful and challenging conflicts. Our profession is highly competitive, competing against each other for both advancement in our firm and new clients.

Demands of Your Partners

Often, no matter what you do, you're expected to do more. The partner gives us more work and is usually unhappy with our work.

Is this a fair summary of what you all encounter? No, of course not, but all of us have experienced at least some of the stresses from time to time.

How Does The Stress You Face As Lawyers Affect You?

Why is stress such a big problem for us? It has many adverse effects on us. When you feel stressed, your muscles tense, your heart beats faster, and you feel tired, anxious, and distracted. It can contribute to many serious health problems, including high blood pressure, heart disease, obesity, stomach issues, and diabetes. And you may eat and sleep poorly. Stress is a leading cause of mental health issues, such as anxiety and depression. Addiction is an all too common problem in our profession.

It affects our relationships. When constantly stressed, you do not show up to your spouse, friends, and family as your best self. Instead, you become irritable and moody and may lose interest in social activities.

Perhaps most significantly, you begin to lose the enjoyment and fulfillment of the profession you had loved for so long. You get burned out. You become physically and emotionally exhausted at work. You are less productive. You are no longer professionally satisfied. Our work performance suffers: you cannot concentrate, you become indecisive, and you cannot effectively manage your caseload. Your judgment may be impaired.

You must manage this stress and prioritize self-care to prevent these adverse effects and maintain your health and well-being.

What Are Helpful Tools To Manage Our Stress?

How do you manage that stress so that you still find your position fulfilling and are successful in what you do? Here are a dozen practical tools you can begin applying in your daily life:

Be Aware of What Stresses You

What situations or circumstances make you feel stressed? Is it a particular person at work? Are there negative thoughts or feelings that enter your mind? Is it something about your physical environment? Does your work schedule stress you? Identify the patterns that cause you stress and how you respond to them. That helps you figure out how to handle those situations better in the future. You will react healthily once you understand precisely what causes your stress.

Start Your Day Right

Try to begin your day with as little stress as possible. Get an early start. Have a good breakfast. Do something relaxing (meditate, read, walk). Prepare for your day. Organize your schedule. Avoid traffic stress if you can. Dress well. If you start the day refreshed, prepared, and relaxed, you'll handle stressful situations better.

Establish Your Boundaries

Maintain boundaries between your work requirements and your personal life. The limits are different for each of us. For example, avoid checking work emails during your family or personal time or answering business calls during your family meal or relaxation time. Avoid unnecessary interruptions at work and instead focus on completing the important task you're working on.

Practice Relaxation Techniques

Try to be mindful and aware of your thoughts and experiences. Deep breathing or meditation practices can help relieve stress. Focus on positive, warm, relaxing images.

Take a break!

Find a break in your schedule during the day to go for a walk, relax, and refocus. Eat a healthy lunch and take a real lunch break. Schedule a daily time to turn off your phone and emails and focus on something positive and relaxing. Take your vacation and make it a respite from work.

Be healthy!

Eat clean and nutritional food. Enjoy exercise and develop your hobbies. Get a good night's sleep. Read or listen to relaxing music. Engage in whatever activity you find fun and relaxing, allowing you to escape from the stress of your work. Regular physical activity can help reduce stress levels by releasing endorphins, natural mood-boosting chemicals in the body.

Change Your Workplace Environment

Make your office as calm and relaxing as you can. Include pictures you like, see if you can have more natural light, use a comfortable chair, or make other changes to relax your workplace. Your office is your second home, and it should be as pleasant, warm, and comfortable as possible.

Socialize

Develop relationships with your associates, partners, and coworkers. Enjoy some social interactions that allow you to relax and build your connections. See those you work with as part of your team working together on a common goal. View them as your teammates instead of a source of conflict or frustration. Nurture your social friendships outside of the office as well. Connecting with colleagues, friends, and family can provide emotional support and help reduce stress.

Organize Yourself

Plan your day and schedule what you're going to do and when. Time blocks your activities. Even schedule such things as lunch and breaks from work. When you plan a time to respond to emails or work on a particular project, make that your sole focus. Organize your office; put away unnecessary papers and files. Too many projects in front of you only make you feel more overwhelmed. Clutter only increases stress.

Discard Your Negative Thoughts and Replace Them With Positive Ones

What you think about has a direct impact on how you feel. Think of something positive instead of focusing on what bothers you in your office. What do you like about your profession, office, and coworkers? Instead of being frustrated about your most recent assignment, see it as an opportunity to learn, grow, and perform. Instead of reflecting on how your partner annoys you, consider his helpful characteristics and how he has helped and trained you. Focus on the positive traits of those you work with instead of the mannerisms that frustrate you.

Get Into Action

Most of us enjoy the work of our profession. I love being a trial lawyer and a family law attorney. I feel energized and enthused when preparing a case, outlining a deposition, or organizing a file for trial. Instead of being stressed about how much you must do, pick and tackle the most critical matter. You will have a feeling of success when you complete that task. You will enjoy the work you just did.

Enjoy the Fulfillment of Our Profession

Most of us are in our profession because we feel genuinely fulfilled by helping and serving others. The reality is you became a lawyer as a way to serve others. Helping others nourishes us. When you're of service, you feel less stress and more fulfillment.

Conclusion

Managing stress is essential to maintain health, well-being, and job performance. By incorporating these tools, you can effectively manage stress and prevent burnout. Lawyers must prioritize their health and well-being, leading to better client service, job satisfaction, and quality of life. By managing stress, you can continue to thrive in your careers and lead fulfilling lives inside and outside the courtroom.

Prison 7: Fear

(Fear No More: Exploring Fear's Influence on Lawyers and Strategies for Overcoming It)

"One of the greatest discoveries a man makes, one of his great surprises, is to find he can do what he was afraid he couldn't do."
–Henry Ford

How serious are you about achieving your dreams?

Are you willing to do what is necessary to earn a partner, go for a raise, seek a new job, or start your firm?

What is your biggest professional goal?

Why have you yet to accomplish it?

For most of us, fear limits us to achieve what you want. You must strive for a professional goal to accomplish it. Why not try? The problem is that our fear can often be unknown and very powerful. You sometimes succumb to it without even knowing. How you respond to fear differentiates you from all the others and sets you on your path to success.

Our profession encounters high-stakes situations, demanding clients, and intense scrutiny, triggering fear and anxiety in even the most seasoned attorneys. Fear can hinder our ability to perform at our best, impede professional growth, and compromise overall well-being.

However, by delving into the roots of these fears and employing effective techniques to navigate them, you can reclaim your power and achieve remarkable success in your career. This chapter analyzes the multifaceted nature of fear within the legal profession, identifies familiar sources of anxiety, and provides actionable advice on how lawyers can conquer their fears and thrive as confident and resilient advocates.

How Does Fear Affect You?

Everyone has professional goals and dreams. Not taking aggressive steps towards achieving them while utilizing excuses is letting fear prevent you from achieving success.

Of course, you know what fear is if you're in the woods and you see a large black bear facing you on your path. You immediately sense a physiological flight or fight response, natural for your survival. But in the professional context, worries and fears are more covert, but the results are the same. You may feel dizzy, sweat, or have a dry mouth. Your muscles get tense, and your heart beats faster. You find yourself distracted, affecting your sleep, experiencing weight gain, and an inhibited ability to function well at work.

Fear has a profound impact on attorneys. These are just some of the ways:

Impaired Decision-Making

Fear can cloud judgment and impair decision-making abilities. You may become hesitant or overly cautious, potentially compromising the effectiveness of your strategies or advice to clients.

Reduced Confidence

Fear erodes confidence, causing doubt of your abilities and the second-guessing of your choices. This lack of confidence can hinder your ability to advocate for clients or assertively present persuasive arguments in court.

Professional Anxiety

Lawyers facing fear may experience anxiety, especially in high-pressure situations such as court hearings or negotiations. This anxiety can manifest as nervousness, trembling, or forgetfulness, ultimately impacting your performance and ability to represent clients effectively.

Procrastination

Fear can lead to procrastination and avoidance behaviors. You may delay or avoid taking on challenging cases, tasks, or responsibilities due to apprehension about potential outcomes or fear of failure.

Increased Stress and Burnout

The constant presence of fear can contribute to elevated stress levels. The demanding nature of the legal profession and the fear of making mistakes or not meeting expectations can lead to burnout, resulting in exhaustion, decreased job satisfaction, and a negative impact on your mental and physical well-being.

Strained Relationships

Fear can strain relationships with clients, colleagues, and even personal connections. You may need help communicating effectively, collaborating, or building rapport when fear inhibits your ability to connect authentically and confidently.

Missed Opportunities for Growth

When fear holds you back, you may miss valuable professional growth and advancement opportunities. Fear can prevent you from seeking new challenges, pursuing innovative strategies, or stepping outside your comfort zone.

Diminished Career Satisfaction

If fear goes unaddressed, it can undermine overall career satisfaction. You may become trapped in a cycle of fear-induced stress, dissatisfaction, and limited professional fulfillment.

Recognizing and addressing fear is crucial to thrive in your career. By actively overcoming fear, you can regain your confidence, make sound decisions, perform at your best, maintain healthier relationships, and find greater fulfillment in the legal profession.

What Are The Most Common Fears Attorneys Face?

These are some of them:

Fear of Failure

Have you ever experienced the fear of making mistakes or failing to meet clients' expectations? The pressure to achieve positive outcomes and the potential consequences of errors can create immense anxiety.

Fear of Judgment

You work in a highly scrutinized and competitive environment where clients, colleagues, judges, and the public constantly evaluate your performance. Fear of being judged negatively can hinder your decision-making and self-expression.

Fear of Uncertainty

The legal landscape is ever-changing, and you must regularly navigate complex and ambiguous situations. The fear of the unknown and the unpredictability of outcomes can cause stress and anxiety.

Fear of Public Speaking

Effective communication is a fundamental skill for lawyers, and public speaking is often a central aspect of your work. Many lawyers experience fear or stage fright when presenting arguments in courtrooms, giving presentations, or addressing large audiences.

Fear of Rejection

Lawyers may face rejection from clients, opposing counsel, or judges. This fear can stem from concerns about needing to be more persuasive, losing a case, or being perceived as inadequate.

Recognizing these common fears is the first step toward addressing and overcoming them. By understanding the specific fears that affect lawyers, you can adopt targeted strategies to manage and conquer these challenges, ultimately fostering personal and professional growth.

What Are The Most Important Benefits of Managing Fears

Overcoming fears can bring numerous benefits, personally and professionally. Here are some of the key advantages:

Increased Confidence

Conquering fears boosts self-assurance and enhances confidence levels. As a lawyer, confidence is vital when presenting arguments, negotiating, or advocating for clients. You can project a more persuasive presence in the courtroom and other legal arenas by overcoming fears.

Improved Performance

Fear can hinder performance by clouding judgment, causing hesitation, and impeding decision-making. You can reach your full potential when you overcome fears, make sounder legal judgments, take calculated risks, and deliver higher-quality work.

Enhanced Professional Growth

Fear often constrains you from pursuing new opportunities, taking on challenging cases, or seeking career advancement. Overcoming fears allows you to step outside your comfort zone, embrace growth opportunities, and expand your professional horizons. You will grow to be more effective.

Effective Communication

Fear can undermine communication, particularly in public speaking or client interactions. You can communicate with greater clarity, eloquence, and confidence by conquering your fears. You can also deliver compelling arguments, connect with clients more deeply, and engage with colleagues more effectively.

Stronger Advocacy

Overcoming fears empowers you to become a stronger client advocate. You can more aggressively present your cases by eliminating fear-induced hesitations, challenging opposing arguments, and asserting your client's rights. You will be a more effective and impactful advocate on behalf of clients.

Stress Reduction and Well-being

Fear can contribute to chronic stress, anxiety, and burnout. Overcoming fears can alleviate stress, promote well-being, and improve work-life balance. When you conquer fears, you manage stress and prioritize self-care, improving physical and mental health.

Enhanced Professional Reputation

Lawyers who exude confidence and fearlessness develop a positive professional reputation. Clients, colleagues, and judges are likelier to view them as competent, reliable, and trustworthy advocates. That reputation can increase referrals, career opportunities, and success.

Personal Empowerment

Overcoming fears is a transformative journey that fosters personal growth and empowerment. By conquering fears, you develop resilience, self-belief, and a sense of control over your professional life. This empowerment extends beyond your legal career, positively influencing your relationships and overall quality of life.

Overcoming fears can have far-reaching benefits, including increased confidence, improved performance, professional growth, effective communication, reduced stress, enhanced reputation, and personal empowerment. By conquering fears, lawyers can unlock their full potential, achieve remarkable success, and thrive in their legal careers.

How Do We Overcome These Fears and Enjoy These Benefits?

Our fears are manageable. Learning how to overcome your fears can help you achieve the life of your dreams. Here are twelve practical steps for you to utilize in conquering your fears:

Identify Your Fears

The first step is recognizing the specific concerns holding you back. Take time to reflect on the root causes of your anxieties and understand how they impact your professional life. Likely, your fear is based on some subconscious feeling you have not considered. Sit quietly. Observe your thoughts, feelings, and sensations. Be mindful of what is at work here. What is it that you're afraid of? Gaining clarity of what is at the center of your fear will help you understand how to defeat it.

Accept Your Feelings

Reflect on them. Simply sit with your fears and understand them. Don't judge yourself; It's normal to feel that way. What is the cause of your worries? What story do you tell yourself about yourself that makes you think you cannot overcome them? Is that story real, and does it serve you?

Seek Support

Contact mentors, colleagues, or professional networks for guidance and support. Sharing your fears with trusted individuals can provide perspective, encouragement, and advice on navigating similar challenges. Your family and best friends will lift you. They want what is best for you. They believe in you, even when you're feeling inadequate. But even better, obtain professional mentoring. A coach can be tremendously helpful in processing what is going on and getting a new perspective.

Embrace Uncertainty

The results are never guaranteed when you try something new or take on a new challenge. The future is unpredictable. That is okay! It's normal to have doubts and be afraid, but you don't want to let that stop you from having the life of your dreams. If you're too comfortable and live in a world of certainty, you will never grow, change, or accomplish something new. Change your perspective on uncertainty. See it as something exciting and refreshing rather than something scary.

Visualize Your Goals

You're trying something new because you're not completely happy with where you are. You want something better for yourself. Fix that goal in your mind. See it. Feel it. Break down your larger goals into smaller, manageable steps. By setting achievable objectives, you can gradually build confidence and momentum, reducing the overwhelming nature of fear. Is it worth challenging your fears to accomplish that dream of your life?

Eliminate Excuses

Fear makes us delay our progress. Sometimes, you cover up fears by making up some excuse that is not real. "I do not have the time." "I am not good enough." "That's not the kind of thing I'm good at." Drop those excuses and take steps to overcome them. If you have identified your fears and understood and accepted them, you know those excuses are simply a way of succumbing to them. Tell your excuses "no," and do not give in to them.

Learn from Setbacks

Accept that setbacks are part of the journey. When facing failures or setbacks, reflect on the lessons learned rather than the negative ones. Use these experiences as opportunities for growth and improvement. Our journey is not about always being successful. It's about growing and changing. Even if you do not achieve your goals on the first attempt, you will have learned new skills and developed more strength from trying. Develop a mindset where you want to grow and become better.

Prepare for Success

Preparation is a powerful antidote to fear. Invest time in thorough research, meticulous case analysis, and well-organized arguments. The more prepared you are, the more confident you'll feel when facing challenging situations. Planning and preparing weaken the fears that are holding you back.

Face Your Fears

Embrace opportunities to confront your fears head-on. Gradually expose yourself to situations that trigger anxiety, such as public speaking or taking on challenging cases. With each experience, you'll build confidence and realize that your fears are often disproportionate to the outcomes.

Stay Present

All too often, our fears involve our projecting ahead into the future. What will they think? What will it mean if I fail? Stop focusing on the future. Stay in the moment. Make your focus on what you're doing rather than what it means. If you stay focused on the present moment, your fears will lose their power.

Get Into Action

Now that you have prepared, understood our fears, and know the next step, let's get started! We know what to do to succeed and have the tools and training to get there. As a trial lawyer, I would have been less effective if I had focused on the case's outcome and what it would mean if I lost. Instead, when I focused on preparing my case, I enjoyed the process and was freed to try the case effectively. We all know what to do. Instead of "worrying" about what it means and what will happen, let's start and take the first steps on our path to success.

Stay Positive

Acknowledge and celebrate your achievements, no matter how small. Recognizing your progress and successes will boost your confidence and reinforce positive habits. Make a conscious decision to develop a mindset of success that you're good enough, have what it takes, and are worth it. When the negative thoughts enter our heads, discard them. Be conscious of your thoughts and make a purposeful decision to choose thoughts of success and optimism rather than ones of failure.

Conclusion

Fear doesn't have to be a hindrance but can catalyze growth and empowerment. By recognizing and addressing our fears head-on, you can unlock our true potential, becoming fearless advocates who confidently navigate the complexities of the legal profession. Remember, conquering fears is not an overnight process but a transformative journey that requires resilience, self-reflection, and a commitment to personal growth. Embrace the challenges, lean into discomfort, and trust in your abilities. Let go of the limiting grip of fear. You can become the attorney you aspire to be – fearless, relentless, and unstoppable. Take that first courageous step and embark on this extraordinary path of fearless advocacy.

Prison 8: People-Pleasing

(The Curse Of People-Pleasing: How To Break Free And Live Authentically)

"I can't tell you the key to success, but the key to failure is trying to please everyone."
– Ed Sheeran

**Have you ever been asked to do something
for someone, said yes, and then resented that
you had to do it?**

**Has someone ever complained about something,
and you said, "I'm sorry," when you did not think
you did anything wrong?**

If so, you may suffer from what is commonly called "people pleasing." It's not bad, but it can lead to frustration, resentment, and losing connection with who you are. Many of us have suffered from people-pleasing. I know I have. In this chapter, you'll learn what people pleasing is, its causes, symptoms, and adverse effects. Most importantly, you'll see the gifts you can receive when you limit this behavior and the tools to overcome it.

What is People Pleasing?

Merriam-Webster defines a "people pleaser" as "someone who has an emotional need to please others, often at the expense of his or her own needs or desires." People who engage in people-pleasing tend to prioritize the needs of others above their own, often to the point where they neglect their own needs and desires. People-pleasing can manifest in different ways, such as constantly seeking approval and validation from others, being overly accommodating, avoiding conflict, and putting others' needs before their own.

A people pleaser is someone you often find appealing, someone who is kind, helpful, considerate, and agreeable. They are the ones who continually step up and say "sure" when someone needs help. If that sounds like you, you may be a people pleaser.

That sounds good, doesn't it? It does, but at some point, constantly making yourself available to others can take an emotional toll. You may neglect your needs because you want to please others when they ask for help.

People pleasers need validation from others to feel good about themselves. They can go to extremes to earn praise from others. The confidence of a people pleaser rises and falls based on how others perceive them. For many, the eagerness to please stems from self-worth issues. They hope that saying yes to everything asked of them will help them feel accepted and liked. Don't all humans want to be liked?

Of course, it's pretty standard to want to make others happy and to be positively regarded. There's nothing inherently wrong with being nice or kind to others. Indeed, it's a valuable trait.

But it can create problems for us when you do it primarily to avoid disappointing others or to make yourself an ideal image. While people-pleasing can stem from a desire to be liked and accepted by others, it can also lead to resentment, burnout, and a loss of one's sense of self. Many people-pleasers purposely choose to do so mainly because they fear upsetting others. It's a great way to avoid conflict, but you will feel drained and unhappy in the long run.

Somewhere along the way, people pleasers decide that everyone else's needs are more important than theirs. They forget their own needs and goals. They then end up feeling resentful, dissatisfied, and depressed. It's hard to be true to yourself when you consistently act based on what you think other people want.

What Are the Causes of People-Pleasing?

Before you can stop being a people-pleaser, you should understand some of the reasons for this behavior. Several factors might play a role, including:

Childhood Experiences

People who grew up in homes with a lot of conflict or criticism may have learned to prioritize other people's needs to avoid conflict or to seek approval.

Poor Self-Esteem

Sometimes, you engage in people-pleasing behavior because you don't value who you are or your desires and needs. Due to a lack of self-confidence, people-pleasers seek external validation. They believe that helping others will lead to approval.

Insecurity

In other cases, you might try to please others because you're concerned that you won't be liked if you do not go the extra mile to make others happy.

Perfectionism

Sometimes, you want everything to be perfect, including how others feel about you.

Past Experiences

Painful or traumatic experiences may also play a role. We may have experienced some events in our lives that caused us to seek approval from others.

Fear of Rejection

People-pleasers may fear being disliked by others, so they go out of their way to avoid conflict and keep everyone happy.

Personality Traits

People who are naturally empathetic to the feelings of others may be more prone to people-pleasing behavior.

People-pleasing behavior is not necessarily a character flaw. Instead, it can be a learned coping mechanism developed in response to various life experiences. However, It's essential for individuals struggling with people-pleasing to learn how to prioritize their needs and create healthy boundaries in their relationships.

What Are the Signs of a People Pleaser?

So how do you know whether you're just a nice person or someone who fits the profile of a people pleaser? It's one thing to want to help others because it's part of your nature. But people-pleasers often end up being taken advantage of by others. Signs you may be a people pleaser include:

Agreeing With Whoever Is In Front Of Us

Agreeability is often a surefire way to win approval. Many politely listen to others because It's a good social practice. However, it can become people-pleasing if you constantly agree with people because you want their approval and not because you believe what you say. Pretending to agree just to be liked can cause us to behave in ways that conflict with our values.

Apologizing For Things That Aren't Our Fault

People pleasers often make themselves responsible for the emotional responses of others. If someone feels bad, you may blame yourself or worry that person thinks you're why they feel bad. Are you always ready with a "sorry!" when something goes wrong? People-pleasers accept blame, even when what happened has nothing to do with them. Whether you excessively blame yourself or worry other people are always blaming you, frequent apologies can be a sign of a bigger problem. It's good to say you're sorry if you hurt someone. But, there's a deeper issue if you frequently apologize for things that were not our responsibility. You don't have to be sorry for being you.

Not Being Able To Say No

You may be a people pleaser if you find it difficult to tell others no when they ask you for something. Do you ever say "yes" to something you do not want to do and resent that you must do it afterward? You might worry that telling someone "no" will make them think you do not care about them. Agreeing to do what they want might seem safer, even if you do not have the time or inclination to help. A pattern of this can cause problems since it tells people their needs come before yours.

Changing Our Personality Depending On Who Is Around Us

People pleasers tend to shift their behavior to match that of the person or group. We act how we think others want us to behave. We act one way with one group of people and a different way with another person. That can lead to behaving in ways that are out of character or participating in unhealthy actions just to fit in socially. People pleasers tend to do anything possible to curry favor, even if it means becoming entirely different.

You Feel Responsible For How Others Feel

It's healthy to recognize your behavior influences others. Thinking you can make someone happy is a problem. It's up to each individual to be in charge of their emotions.

You Feel Uncomfortable If Someone Is Angry At You

People-pleasing tends to involve a fear of anger. Of course, just because someone is upset doesn't necessarily mean you did anything wrong. But you may be more likely to compromise your values if you cannot tolerate the thought that someone is upset with you.

Constantly Seeking Validation

You may need approval from others and base your self-worth on their opinions of you. Some of us need praise to feel good. While kind words make us all feel good, people pleasers need validation. If our self-worth rests entirely on what others think about us, we will feel good only when others compliment us.

Fear Of Conflict Or Criticism

You may avoid conflict or criticism and go to great lengths to avoid upsetting or disappointing others, even if it means suppressing your needs and desires. It's one thing not to want to start a fight. But avoiding conflict at all costs means you'll struggle to stand up for who and what you believe in.

Difficulty Expressing Your True Thoughts And Feelings

You may find it difficult to express your true thoughts, feelings, and opinions, especially if it might upset or disappoint others. You don't admit when your feelings are hurt. We cannot form genuine relationships with people unless we're willing to speak up and say our feelings are hurt. Denying that you're hurt, sad, embarrassed, or disappointed — when you're emotionally wounded — harms our relationships and ourselves.

Putting Others' Needs Before Your Own

You may prioritize the needs and wants of others before your own, even if it means sacrificing your time, energy, and resources.

Feeling Guilty When You Can't Please Others

You may feel guilty or anxious when you can't fulfill the expectations or requests of others, even if it's not reasonable or healthy for you to do so.

Feeling Drained Or Burnt Out

You may feel exhausted, drained, or burnt out from constantly trying to please others and neglecting your needs and well-being.

You may struggle with people-pleasing tendencies if you resonate with some or all of these signs.

Effects of Being a People-Pleaser

If you're in constant people-pleaser mode, you can lose sight of who you are. You may have no idea of what truly makes you happy. People-pleasing isn't inherently harmful, but trying to earn the regard of others usually means you neglect your own needs and feelings. In a way, you're putting on an act. You're doing what you think people want so they like you. You might only pretend to enjoy helping since this is part of keeping people happy. This isn't strictly honest; people-pleasing can hurt you and your relationships over time.

Constant people-pleasing behavior can lead to:

Lack Of Self-Care

Constantly devoting yourself to meeting the needs of others can cause you to neglect your own. As a result, you may get sick or mentally burned out from the pressure of trying to please everyone.

Built-Up Resentment

You may be bottling up anger because you feel people take advantage of you. That can lead you to make passive-aggressive comments and show your frustration. As a result, you may isolate yourself from people instead of letting them know what's going on and working to improve the situation.

Anger and Frustration

While you might enjoy helping, you're also bound to experience frustration when doing things out of obligation. These feelings can lead to a cycle of helping someone, feeling mad at them for taking advantage, and then feeling sorry for yourself.

Anxiety and Stress

Efforts to keep others happy can stretch your physical and mental resources too thin. Trying to manage it all can leave you plagued with anxiety, which can harm your health.

Depleted Willpower

Devoting all your energy and mental resources toward making sure others are happy means you're less likely to have the resolve and willpower to tackle your goals.

Lack of Authenticity

People-pleasers often hide their own needs and preferences to accommodate other people. As a result, you may need to live authentically or lose touch with who you are – constantly putting others' needs before oneself can lead to losing identity and a lack of direction.

Weaker Relationships

Healthy relationships are balanced and involve give-and-take. You do nice things for loved ones, and they do the same for you. You probably won't have very fulfilling relationships when people like you only because you do nice things for them. You may feel resentful if you put all your efforts into ensuring you meet other people's expectations. While people might appreciate your giving nature, they may also begin to take your kindness for granted.

People Take Advantage Of You

People-pleasers often have difficulty setting boundaries and saying no, which can lead to being taken advantage of by others. Some people will quickly recognize and take advantage of people-pleasing tendencies. They may not be able to name the behavior. But they know you'll agree to whatever they ask, so they'll keep asking. And you keep saying yes because you want to keep them happy. But this can seriously affect your time, finances, and emotional well-being.

Burnout

One massive impact of people-pleasing is burnout. This can quickly happen when you take on more than you can handle for others. You don't just lose out on time for yourself. You also have less time for things you need to do. To get the bare essentials taken care of, you might end up working longer hours or going without sleep, eventually facing physical consequences of worry and stress.

Difficulty Making Decisions

People-pleasers often struggle to make decisions because they are so focused on what others want. What do they want? What should I do? This creates confusion and uncertainty.

People-pleasing can be problematic when it becomes a habitual pattern that interferes with our ability to live a fulfilling life and prioritize our needs and goals.

What Are The Gifts Of Overcoming People Pleasing?

Overcoming people-pleasing can have many benefits, including:

Improved Self-Esteem

Overcoming people-pleasing can help you build a stronger self-worth and confidence. You can see yourself deserving of respect and care by prioritizing your needs and desires.

Healthier Relationships

When you can set boundaries and communicate your needs effectively, you can build healthier relationships with others. Boundaries can lead to more fulfilling connections with friends, family, and romantic partners.

More Authenticity

People-pleasers often struggle to express their true feelings and desires. Overcoming people-pleasing can help you become more authentic to yourself, which can be empowering and fulfilling.

Greater Sense of Control

When you stop focusing on pleasing others, you can regain control over your life. You can decide based on what is best for you rather than trying to please everyone else.

Reduced Stress and Anxiety

People-pleasing can be exhausting and stressful, leading to anxiety and burnout. By learning to prioritize your own needs and set boundaries, you can reduce stress and improve your overall well-being.

Overcoming people-pleasing can lead to greater self-awareness, healthier relationships, and a more fulfilling and authentic life.

How Do We Break Out of the Prison of People Pleasing?

When people-pleasers recognize the traps they set for themselves, it becomes easier to avoid those old habits in favor of new ones. So, how do you break out of this prison? Here are 14 tangible tips:

Identify Your Values

Take time to identify your values and priorities. You can then make decisions and set boundaries that align with your values rather than just trying to please others.

Practice Mindfulness

Mindfulness can help you become more aware of your thoughts, feelings, and behaviors and help you identify people-pleasing patterns. Try practicing mindfulness meditation, yoga, or other mindful activities.

Develop Healthy Communication Skills

Communicating assertively and respectfully can help you set boundaries and healthily express your needs and wants. Take time to practice active listening, speaking clearly, and using "I" instead of "you" statements.

Learn to say "NO."

Sometimes, people-pleasing can become such a deeply ingrained habit that you must tell yourself that It's okay to say "no." For example, it's okay to put yourself first and say "no" if someone asks you for something you don't want to do. Start getting out of the people-pleasing habit by saying no to something small. You must also stop saying "yes" just because the other person asks for help. The most important part about this is reminding yourself that saying "no" when you mean it isn't being selfish; it's taking care of yourself.

Set Healthy Boundaries

People-pleasers often need to be made aware of the limits they need to set. Boundaries allow you to say "no" when someone asks for help or takes advantage of your time. Remember, you're not selfish—you're just confident enough in who you are that you understand you do not have to agree with someone's requests all the time.

You Can't Please Everyone

It's a tough pill to swallow, but you must understand that you can't make everybody happy. The simple truth is that you can't always please everyone because people's needs are different from person to person. Acting to please one person may upset or offend someone else. Instead, try to work authentically, and people who like the true you will appreciate you for who you are.

Be Assertive

Learn to stand up for yourself. There are times when people don't know that they're bothering you. They might be your friends or family and have good intentions. But if you've had enough, it's time to take a stand. It's important not to let others dictate how you live and feel about yourself. Being assertive will help you set boundaries and ensure that others around you respect those boundaries.

Accept Yourself

People-pleasers often have high expectations and can be hard on themselves when they make mistakes. Practice self-compassion by treating yourself with kindness, understanding, and forgiveness. When you give in to people-pleasing, you lose touch with who you are. You start to believe that your value can be measured by what other people think of you. But this is not the case. Stop caring what others think of you and fully accept yourself as you are. Part of accepting yourself is acknowledging and using your strengths. When you accept yourself for who you are, everyone else will eventually follow suit.

Be More Honest About Your Feelings

Being honest is the best policy! You'll face rejection at some point in life and should be ready for that. However, if you're honest with people, it will open up new doors for you.

Make Yourself The Priority

It's about understanding what you want from life, prioritizing it, and not placing other people's desires first. You should prioritize yourself by putting your needs first, even if that means disappointing someone else who has asked something of you that feels like more than you can handle.

Check Your Motives

Are you acting a certain way, saying yes, or being agreeable to win favor or please others? Or are you doing what you want? Is it consistent with your values, goals, and beliefs? Help when you want to help. You don't need to give up being kind and thoughtful. Those are desirable qualities that can contribute to solid and lasting relationships. The key is to examine your intentions. Don't do things only because you fear rejection or want the approval of others.

Set Your Personal Goals
Consider where you want to spend your time. Who do you want to help? What goals are you trying to accomplish? Knowing your priorities can help you determine whether or not you have the time and energy to devote to something.

Reflect Before Responding
If someone asks for a favor, tell them you need time to consider it. Say something like, "I don't know; let me think about it. I will get back to you." Saying "yes" right away can leave you feeling obligated and overcommitted, but taking your time to respond to a request can give you the time to evaluate it and decide if it's something you want to do.

Build A Support System
Surround yourself with people who support your goals and values and encourage you to prioritize your needs. A positive community can help you see your truth and be committed to your values.

Defeating people-pleasing is a process that takes time and effort. Be patient with yourself, and celebrate small victories along the way. You can develop healthy habits and live a more authentic and fulfilling life with practice.

Conclusion

Overcoming people-pleasing can be challenging, but it is worth it. By prioritizing your needs and desires, you can build a stronger sense of self-worth and confidence, develop healthier relationships, and live a more authentic and fulfilling life. Remember that this takes time and effort and may involve setbacks. But with patience, self-compassion, and determination, you can break free from the patterns that hold you back and discover the joy and empowerment of living life on your terms. So take that first step today and begin the journey towards a happier, more fulfilling life.

Prison 9: Other People's Opinions

(Lawyers Unleashed: How To Embrace Resilience Against Others' Opinions)

"When we liberate ourselves from the opinion of others, we become genuinely powerful."
– Avijeet Das

Do you spend too much energy wondering what others think about you?

Do you worry that others might judge you because of something you're doing or undertaking?

Are you afraid to take on a new challenge because you wonder what others will think of you?

How does that make you feel?

I know I have. I've often worried about what others think of me and what opinions they hold of me. This is a pervasive problem for many of us, but is unhealthy. And you do have it within your power to escape from this prison.

In the demanding world of law, the ability to remain unfazed by the opinions of others is a valuable skill for lawyers. We navigate a landscape where our decisions and actions are subject to constant scrutiny and critique. Yet, succumbing to the weight of external opinions can hinder our effectiveness and compromise our mental well-being.

Therefore, you must develop tools and strategies to rise above the noise, maintain your composure, and focus on your legal responsibilities. By cultivating resilience, practicing self-validation, and embracing a healthy perspective on criticism, you can shield yourself from the potentially harmful effects of others' opinions and ensure you perform at your best.

In this chapter, you'll learn why humans worry so much about what others think, discuss some of the problems it causes, explain why other people's opinions don't matter, and gain tangible tools to start living your life free of the opinions of others.

Why Do You Care So Much What Others Think of You?

We all crave a human connection with other people. Given a choice, does it not make sense that you would prefer to be liked by those around you rather than disliked? The quality and depth of our relationships with those we care about can affect our true happiness. Social media drives this in part. Some think the number of likes on a post somehow reflects how accepted you are.

Approval from others can also give us a higher sense of self-esteem. We believe that recognition and approval of others affect our self-worth and how we value ourselves.

And, it does make sense to act appropriately, speak respectfully, dress nicely, and be kind and courteous. Those are all good things. And they do affect what other people think of us. But fear can cause us to act this way. We fear you will need more friends or intimate connections.

Insecurity can make us crave acceptance from others. Often, we care so much about other people's opinions of us because we feel what other people think of us determines our self-worth. When you look good in their eyes, you feel better about yourself. Too often, we live our lives based on what others think of us instead of how we are.

Our role as lawyers makes this common human dilemma even harder.
We can be particularly affected by the opinions of others for these reasons:

Reputation And Professional Image
You have worked so hard to establish a positive reputation among your peers. Negative opinions or criticisms can be perceived as a threat to your professional image, causing you to feel defensive about your standing in the legal profession.

Client Satisfaction And Outcomes
Attorneys are committed to providing excellent representation and achieving favorable outcomes for clients. You may take it personally and doubt your abilities when they express disappointment or dissatisfaction.

Validation and Self-Worth
Like anyone else, lawyers seek recognition for their work. When your efforts face criticism or negative opinions, it can impact your sense of self-worth and lead to feelings of self-doubt.

Fear Of Judgment And Professional Consequences
You work in environments where your partners, colleagues, judges, or juries scrutinize your performance. The fear of adverse judgments or repercussions, such as professional setbacks or damage to your career trajectory, can contribute to heightened sensitivity towards others' opinions.

Personal Investment
Attorneys are deeply involved in our client's emotional, intellectual,

and often financial situations. You spend significant time, energy, and empathy to further your client's interests. Consequently, you may struggle to separate yourself when your efforts are criticized or disapproved.

Perfectionism and High Standards

You likely commit to high standards of excellence and sometimes may have a perfectionistic streak. Consequently, you're more prone to internalizing criticism as you strive for flawless performance and fear falling short of your expectations.

The Problems With Worrying About What Other People Think Of You

You should be the captain of your life and choose to live it as you want. When you worry about what others think of you, you may live in fear and waste some of your opportunities. All the great things you can accomplish sit in the background because you fear rejection or judgment.

There are many reasons why you should stop worrying about other people's opinions:

Giving Up Control

When you give emotional energy to worry about what other people think of you, it gives them power over you. Do they deserve that? Or want it? Of course not. Your life is yours to live.

Life Becomes Small

When you worry about what others think of you, you may pass on opportunities, and your world shrinks. You may live in regret that you didn't choose to pursue some possible avenue for success.

Others May Not Even Be Thinking About You

You may be amazed at how little others think about you. And you do not know their opinions or what they are thinking. It's easy to imagine negative thoughts and use them to avoid pursuing something because of fear. But those negative opinions may not even exist.

More Stress

When you worry about the opinions of others, you simply create anxiety in your lives for no reason. We do not know their opinions, and their opinions do not matter, yet you waste precious time worrying about them.

Dream Stealers

Those with negative thoughts about us often act out of jealousy and Insecurity. We have dreams and a vision of success. They often, sometimes unconsciously, do not want us to succeed. Should you allow them to kill our dreams?

If you're true to yourself, the opinions of others simply do not matter. If you live a good life, do what is right, and stand up for your beliefs, the opinions of others have no importance whatsoever.

How Does Worrying About Others' Opinions Affect Lawyers?

As lawyers, the problems go deeper. When you excessively worry about others' opinions, you face several problems that negatively impact your professional life:

Impaired Decision-Making

Constantly seeking approval or fearing disapproval can lead to decision-making paralysis. We hesitate to take necessary risks or make bold choices out of fear of how others perceive us. This can hinder our ability to advocate effectively for our clients and make sound legal judgments.

Increased Stress and Anxiety

Excessive concern about others' opinions can contribute to

heightened stress levels and chronic anxiety. We may constantly feel the pressure to meet external expectations, leading to burnout and negative impacts on our mental and physical well-being.

Inconsistent Self-Image

Relying too heavily on others' opinions can result in an inconsistent sense of self. We may struggle to maintain a stable self-identity, constantly adjusting our behavior and views based on the feedback we receive. This can lead to a need for more authenticity.

Loss of Confidence and Self-Esteem

When you place excessive value on external validation, your self-confidence can be easily shaken when faced with criticism or disapproval. This can erode our belief in our abilities, diminish self-esteem, and create a constant need for reassurance from others.

Professional Stagnation

We may become risk-averse and hesitant to try new approaches or innovative strategies when preoccupied with others' opinions. This can hinder our professional growth, limit our ability to adapt to changing legal landscapes, and ultimately impede our career advancement.

Loss of Authenticity and Values Alignment

Constantly seeking validation from others can cause us to compromise our authenticity and suppress our true beliefs or values. We may prioritize conforming to external expectations rather than staying true to our principles. As a result, you may feel unfulfilled.

Why Do Other People's Opinions Of Us Not Matter?

We sometimes waste so much energy and create so much stress worrying about what other people think of us, and in truth, their opinions do not matter for many reasons:

Gossipers Always Gossip

Some people simply like to express opinions about others. That is how they make themselves feel better. They always talk about others. You're not the only one they talk about. It's their habit. And it's not healthy.

What's Good For Them May Not Be Good For You

Everyone is unique. You have your talents and opportunities, your vision. Those who have opinions of us may be in an entirely different place in their life. What may work for them may not work for us. What they want to accomplish in their life may be completely different than your dreams for yourself.

It's Our Life And Our Journey

You're in control of our choices and actions. We should not let others control our journey.

You Can't Please Everyone

I certainly tried. It's never possible to please all the people all the time. It only creates frustration and disappointment.

Others Do Not Determine Our Self-Worth

Instead, it comes from who you are, your beliefs and values, how you act consistently with them, and how much energy and commitment you put forth in life. What others think of you doesn't determine who you are or where you end up.

What Are Some Tools For Lawyers To Not Let Other People's Opinions Affect Them?

It's not easy to break this habit, but It's within our control. We can break out of the prison of worrying about the opinions of other people by trying these handy tools:

Understand That Hurt People Hurt People

Sometimes, those who express negative opinions of us do it only because of their issues, problems, or pain. They often say what they say is not about us but about them and their obstacles. Once you understand that, It's easier not to let them bother you.

Opinions Don't Matter

Realize that those who express opinions about us will never be helpful to us. If It's our goal to accomplish our dreams, those who are open to telling us why we should not simply will never help us be successful. Their thoughts and opinions do not serve us. Therefore, we should not give them any space in our heads.

Let Go

Let those with opinions have them, but simply let go of them. Accept those people as who they are, but do not allow them to control your happiness or actions. They must understand who you are and what you're trying to accomplish. Their opinions have little to do with you and much more about themselves.

Stop Comparing

All too often, you worry about the opinions of others because you're comparing yourself to them. This is our life, not theirs. We all have our gifts, talents, and challenges. Comparison only creates envy and disappointment. It doesn't support us on our journey.

Stay Positive

Do not give in to negativity. Surround yourself with those who support you. Having positive thoughts and a support system will help you succeed.

Celebrate Your Successes

Each night, write in your journal any good things that happened to you today, any win, every positive result, anything of which you're proud or gave you a sense of accomplishment. You'll soon see that good things consistently happen when you focus on yourself and your activity. You develop a stronger sense of self-worth and confidence by acknowledging your achievements. Recognizing your accomplishments counterbalances any negative opinions and criticism.

Practice Self-Acceptance

You're unique and special. You have skills, experiences, and talents that no one else does. Learn to love and accept who you are. Forgive yourself for any failings, but learn from them. Always remember that you're a gift to the world and have much you can accomplish.

Be Self-Aware

Self-awareness is crucial for lawyers to understand their triggers and emotional responses to external opinions. By being aware of our thoughts and feelings, we can better manage and regulate our emotions.

Healthy Boundaries

Establishing healthy emotional and professional boundaries is essential. Lawyers should recognize that you cannot please everyone and that your self-worth doesn't solely rely on external validation. Setting clear boundaries with clients, colleagues, and even personal connections can help protect our mental and emotional well-being.

Support Networks

Building a solid support network, including mentors, colleagues, and trusted friends or family members, can provide lawyers with a safe space for discussing concerns, seeking guidance, and receiving constructive feedback. Surrounding oneself with supportive individuals can counterbalance the impact of negative opinions.

Conclusion

Lawyers must recognize the immense value of not allowing the opinions of others to consume them. By embracing your inner strength and resilience, you can safeguard your decision-making, preserve your mental well-being, and maintain authenticity. Through self-awareness, mindfulness, and constructive feedback evaluation, you can filter out unwarranted criticism and focus on your professional growth. You can rise above external judgments and foster a fulfilling legal career by setting healthy boundaries, seeking support networks, and celebrating your achievements. Remember that the path to success lies not in appeasing every opinion but in remaining steadfast, confident, and committed to your journey.

Prison 10: Comparison

(Stop Comparing, Start Living: Strategies for a More Authentic Life)

"Comparison is the thief of joy."
– Theodore Roosevelt

Do you ever do this?

You see someone proficient, better than you, at something you want to achieve, and you compare yourself to them.

You want to be better in your profession, so it makes sense to compare yourself to the best, doesn't it?

How does that work out for you?

How does it make you feel?

In today's world, where social media and other platforms allow us to compare ourselves with others constantly, it's all too easy to fall into the trap of comparison. While comparing yourself with others may seem harmless initially, it can quickly become a source of stress, anxiety, and low self-esteem. Furthermore, constantly measuring yourself against others can lead to unhealthy competition, jealousy, and a distorted sense of self-worth. Fortunately, there are strategies to overcome the comparison problem and cultivate a healthier, more positive mindset. This chapter explores the issues and offers tangible tools to help you break free from the comparison trap and focus on your unique journey.

The Trouble With Comparisons

Comparison truly is the thief of joy. When you compare yourself to others, you're looking up at someone extraordinarily gifted at something in which you have yet to be. So you're looking at their best side, not noticing the weaknesses and failures. It's comparing their best to an area where you need to grow, hoping to learn from the comparison, but often thwarting your success.

These are some of the problems with comparing yourself with others:

Kills Confidence

When you compare an area of weakness with someone else's absolute best, you inevitably think, "I can never do that." Instead of learning from the experience of others, you begin to question your ability to succeed. We destroy our vision of success. If you compare yourself to the best in your profession, you think you will never be that good. We damage our confidence along with our chances of success. Constantly comparing yourself with others can lead to feelings of inadequacy, low self-esteem, and self-doubt.

Envy and Depression

It's effortless to fall victim to jealousy when you look at someone else's success and wish you had it or feel depressed that you have been unable to accomplish the same thing. Comparison can create a very negative mindset, which hinders our ability to succeed.

It's Misleading

We only have part of the picture. You're looking at someone's highlight reel. We do not see their failures, weaknesses, and fears. Therefore, comparing yourself with others can lead to an inaccurate assessment of your abilities and accomplishments, harming your growth and development.

Turns Friends Into Rivals

We can't help but start to compete subconsciously with a successful person. We want to be as good as that person. If you start comparing, you begin living in rivalry and conflict. We may become overly competitive, which can be unhealthy.

Hinders Success

Comparing yourself to someone else who has more friends, a bigger home, a more excellent car, or is more successful professionally only saps our motivation. It decreases our chance to accomplish our goals because we see ourselves as not good enough.

Nothing good ever comes from such comparisons. Overall, comparing yourself with others can harm your well-being and personal growth. Instead, let's focus on our unique qualities and goals and avoid the comparison trap.

A War Story

I have often struggled with comparison in parts of my life. I have been a competitive golfer and am passionate about the sport. I played for my high school and college teams and have competed in club tournaments since. However, I have never been a long hitter of the golf ball. My drives are frequently well short of my opponents, and they hit their irons so much further.

If I hit my drive down the middle, but my opponent hits his 40 yards past me, and I begin to reflect on what a disadvantage I face and how I wish I hit the ball as far as he did, I just put additional pressure on myself. I develop a negative attitude that hinders my success. If my competitor hits a 9 iron on a par 3, and I have to use a 6 iron, and I think about how much longer he is, I believe I'm not as good. Those thoughts will deflate me.

Instead, I should focus on my strengths. I should remember that I hit the ball straighter and more consistently and have a better short game. Concentrating on what I do well makes me more confident and more likely to succeed. Then, when I win the hole, even though my opponent outhit me by 40 yards, he is the one who feels frustrated.

To become a longer golf ball driver, I can seek a coach to help improve my techniques to hit the ball further. And I can continue to work on my strengths and make them better. Comparing my game's weakest part to my opponent's strongest part harms me. On the contrary, focusing on my strengths and goals creates a vision of success that makes me more fulfilled.

Tools to Stop Comparing and Start Living

So, if comparison robs us of our happiness and holds us back from achieving our goals, how do you stop comparing and start living the life of our dreams? Here are some tangible suggestions:

Ask For Guidance From a Trusted Mentor

While you do not want to compare yourself to others, there are valuable resources you can tap into. There are sources of support in our life who want us to succeed, who have done before what we're trying to do now, who are experts in their field, and who are willing to give of themselves to help us succeed. For example, I had the gift of a trusted friend and mentor who taught me how to be a top-notch family lawyer. I didn't compare myself to him; I didn't want to be him, but I wanted to learn from him what he knew. And he taught me how to be successful as a family lawyer.

Celebrate the Success of Others

Instead of feeling jealous when others succeed at something or have something you want, be grateful for their success. Congratulate them. Support them. Besides being nice to someone who is a friend or acquaintance, you free yourself from any feeling of envy that holds you back from being as completely free as you want.

Focus on Your Goals

Instead of obsessing over what someone else has, focus on your goals and vision for your future. What do you want to accomplish? Where do you want to be? What do you need to change to get there? What are the tangible steps you can follow to achieve that? This directs your thinking to something positive. Instead of comparing yourself with others, focus on your journey and progress. Celebrate your successes and accomplishments, and set goals that are meaningful and relevant to you.

Develop Self-Compassion

Self-compassion involves treating yourself with kindness, understanding, and acceptance, even when life is complicated. Practice self-compassion by speaking to yourself in a positive, supportive way and recognizing that making mistakes is a natural part of the learning process.

Cultivate Positive Relationships

Surround yourself with people who support and encourage you and help you feel good about yourself. Positive relationships can help boost your self-esteem and provide a sense of belonging and connection.

Practice Mindfulness

Mindfulness involves being fully present and aware of the moment without judgment or distraction. Practicing mindfulness can help you stay grounded and centered and reduce the temptation to compare yourself with others.

Inventory Your Strengths and Weaknesses

Analyze yourself. Become aware of who you are, what you're good at, and what areas you can improve. What skills do you have that will help you accomplish your goals? What do you need to develop to be successful?

Evaluate Your Growth

Instead of comparing yourself to others, compare yourself to yourself! Where were you a year ago? How have you grown and changed? What goals do you set for yourself that you have accomplished? Where did you fall short? How far have you come, and how far do you have to go? You should only compare yourself to your "past you."

Practice Gratitude

We can spend all the time you want thinking about what you do not have and wish you had. That doesn't serve us well. It creates frustration, disappointment, and envy. Instead, think of the many gifts and blessings that you have. What do you have to be grateful for? What skills do you have that serve us? What do you have in your life that truly is a gift? When you have an attitude of gratitude, you no longer compare yourself to others from a perspective of jealousy; instead, you celebrate their success. You also focus on how you can improve and achieve your goals. Gratitude can help shift your focus from what you lack to what you have. Take time each day to reflect on the things you're grateful for, and make a conscious effort to appreciate the blessings in your life.

Using these tools and strategies, you can break free from the comparison trap and cultivate a healthier, more positive mindset. Remember that everyone has their unique journey, and your worth and value are not determined by how you measure up to others.

Conclusion

The comparison problem is pervasive and can severely affect our well-being and personal growth. By constantly measuring yourself against others, you can become trapped in a cycle of self-doubt, jealousy, and unhealthy competition. However, using the tools and strategies outlined above, you can break free from the comparison trap and cultivate a more positive, authentic, and fulfilling life.

Remember that your worth and value are not determined

by how you measure up to others and that your unique journey should be celebrated, not compared. The only person you should be comparing yourself to is yourself. Your efforts should focus on growing from within, working hard, improving, becoming more resilient, and being grateful. By focusing on your growth, practicing self-compassion, and cultivating positive relationships, you can overcome the problem of comparison and live a more joyful, purposeful life.

Let go of comparison and fuel your success.

Prison 11: Expectations

*"My happiness grows in direct proportion to my acceptance
and in inverse proportion to my expectations."*
– Michael J. Fox

**Do you ever find that you expect a particular result,
like winning your trial, and when it doesn't happen,
you're crushed and disappointed?**

**Alternatively, you win that case that you should
win. Do you not feel less gratitude for the successful
result because you expected it?**

That's the problem with expectations. They can remove the joy from our lives and create disappointment and frustration. In this chapter, I explain the problem with expectations and specific areas that can create problems for us. Finally, I share my experiences and provide tangible tips to help navigate this intricate terrain.

The Problem with Expectations

Expectations are the beliefs you hold about the outcome of certain events. "Expectations" are what you believe will happen, and reality is what transpires. Often, they do not match up. This conflict between reality and our expectations can create both discontentment and unhappiness. When our expectations are not met, it can lead to frustration and even anger. In addition, when what you expect to occur does occur, you do not experience the true exhilaration of the experience precisely because you were expecting it to happen.

Expectations are different from having a confident vision of our success. Having a positive image of our lives and believing in our success is a positive attribute that helps us to achieve our goals. But expectations can be a trap that hinders our success.

Three types of expectations:

1. What you expect of yourself
2. What you expect of others
3. What others expect of you

You have no control over what others expect of you. We each have a life to live, and you can choose your desired path. But you have control over your expectations, both of yourself and others.

Expectations can be compelling with others who do not respond to us as you expect. We do something very nice for someone and do not receive our anticipated appreciation. We hoped to have a good evening with someone, and instead, they were pretty angry and distant. When you have expectations of other people in our lives, you experience disappointment when they do not respond as you thought they would.

Expectations are also problematic with results in our lives. We anticipate a particular outcome from our efforts, but it doesn't materialize. You lose the trial you expected to win or do not receive the raise you expected to receive.

You'll know that your expectations are becoming too powerful when you feel true disappointment when the expected outcome did not occur or you're not adequately grateful for the desired result. A simple example would be a football game. If our team is two touchdown favorites over the opponents yet loses, you're crushed and highly disappointed because you expected them to win. But you're not excited if the good guys win because you expected that to happen. Our expectations can rob us of fully appreciating the experiences in our lives.

Problem Areas For Lawyers

We all know how stressful the practice of law is. When you expect results from other people, you only make it worse. These expectations can crop up in several different areas, including:

The Outcome of the Case

We have a case in which you have worked hard, done a great job, have all the evidence lined up, and expect to win. Surprisingly, the jury ruled against us.

Our Firm

We have put our heart and soul into working hard for our firm, working long hours, and delivering outstanding results. Yet, you do not receive the support, acknowledgment, and financial rewards that you think you deserve.

Your Clients

We work very hard for our clients to deliver what you think are excellent results, yet they are not satisfied and express disappointment about the outcome, how long it took, or how much it cost. Or, you receive a significant settlement offer that you present to the client and expect him to accept, but he doesn't. In addition, clients may complain about not hearing from us faster or more often and need help understanding our workload.

The Court

The court denies a request for a postponement that you should receive. The trial judge ruled against us on a motion when you expected a favorable decision.

Other Lawyers

We ask for a scheduling change for personal reasons, and you expect opposing counsel to agree, but he doesn't. We hope opposing counsel will be professional in their communications with us, but they won't answer calls, call our client names, or are extremely difficult.

Work-Life Balance

If you work hard during the week, are productive, and get a lot done, you hope the weekends will be yours to enjoy with your family. Yet, at the last minute, another matter is dumped on you, preventing us from enjoying the weekend with family as expected.

These are just a few areas where our expectations can cause additional stress in our legal practice. The good news is you can manage those expectations.

My Story

I have struggled with expectations for much of my life. I expected to win the trial. I expected others to act toward me a certain way. I expected to win a golf match. I expected good weather when we went to the football game. All of those combined created disappointment when the reality differed from my expectations.

After years of frustration and disappointment, I learned that my expectations only hurt me. Through my experiences, I have learned various helpful tools for managing our expectations so you can enjoy true personal freedom.

I have learned that the greater my expectations, the more I experience disappointment and frustration. On the other hand, when I do not go through life expecting a specific result or a particular response from other people, I experience much more significant serenity and peace.

Nine Tips for Managing Expectations

How can you control your expectations to not wallow in frustration and disappointment when the anticipated outcome doesn't occur? Here are some tips:

Self-Reflection

Become aware of your expectations. What are your expectations of others? Your spouse, your children? Are they realistic? What about your career? Review your goals and visions, and make sure they are reasonable and measurable. Having unreasonable expectations of others or yourself will lead to disappointment and regret.

Expect the Unexpected

Once you understand that the unexpected is often likely to happen, you can adjust to it more easily. When things go wrong, situations change, or some unanticipated hurdle crops up, take a breath, pause, and consider your best options. The unexpected will happen, more often than not. Life is unpredictable. You can only control your thoughts, feelings, and actions.

Set Boundaries

Let your clients know your time frames and availability. Let your firm understand what your workload and time limitations are. Lawyers must set boundaries and manage others' availability and response time expectations.

Stop Comparing

Sometimes, a source of disappointment is that you expect to achieve what others appear to have. Don't forget that what you see on social media isn't necessarily the life they're living. Comparing yourself to others limits your performance. You may feel envious and disappointed that you don't have what someone else does. To avoid this, set personal goals for yourself without comparison to anyone else.

Live and Let Live

Maybe you don't realize it, but you may sit in judgment of others, how they dress, what they say, how they behave, and their level of success. Let go of your expectations of others, particularly how you want them to respond. They have their own life to live and issues to manage.

Don't Judge Yourself Too Harshly

Sometimes, the expectation problem is when the anticipated result doesn't happen, and you engage in excessive self-criticism. We harshly criticize ourselves for failure and are disappointed we did not live up to our dreams. You're not a failure simply because your expectations did not materialize. Instead, see what you can learn from our setbacks. What lessons are there in the reality that you experienced?

Practice Emotional Acceptance

Life only sometimes works out the way you expected. There will be obstacles. Accepting the outcome is your reality. Your role is to take the reality you face as being precisely what it is supposed to be at that time. Then, decide how you want to respond and move forward.

Be Grateful

You don't always get what you want. Sometimes, you fall short. But you will feel much more fulfilled if you find contentment and truly savor what you have. Happiness doesn't come from getting what you want but from wanting what you have. The most excellent antidote to unrealized expectations is gratitude. Genuinely appreciate the many gifts and blessings in your life. Look for the lesson in the disappointment, then reflect on all you have to be grateful for. If this route did not succeed, consider what course may work out better next time.

Seek Support

Expectations can create resentment and frustration. Find a trusted person to talk to about your situation. A wise, confidential mentor can be a tremendous resource for you. You can receive support, encouragement, understanding, and clarity.

Conclusion

True personal freedom comes from accepting the reality of your situation and being grateful for your gifts. When you live in gratitude, your reality might exceed your expectations in ways you have never expected. Life can become more exciting, new, and wonderful. Powerful expectations can imprison you, but when you let go of them, you can experience more personal freedom. And isn't that what you want, what you deserve?

Prison 12: Limiting Beliefs

(DEFYING DOUBT: EMPOWERING LAWYERS TO OVERCOME LIMITING BELIEFS)

"The only thing limiting you is yourself."
– Ken Poirot

Did you consider trying something new and tell yourself you were not good enough?

Did you have an opportunity to speak or present but tell yourself you would fail?

Do you see a mistake as a catastrophic failure rather than a learning opportunity?

Do you hesitate to take a risk because you fear failure?

So often, you can struggle with limiting beliefs. You may tell yourself a story to explain why you should not try something new. We fear failing, so we use our limiting beliefs as protection. The trouble is that limiting beliefs prevent us from accomplishing our goals. They stop us from being as fulfilled and happy as we want. You can overcome them.

In the demanding world of law, where the stakes are high and the pressure relentless, you often battle both external challenges and the internal obstacles of your limiting beliefs. These self-imposed barriers can silently undermine your confidence, hinder your professional growth, and diminish your ability to reach your full potential. However, recognizing and overcoming these limiting beliefs is not only possible but crucial for lawyers to thrive in their careers. This chapter delves into conquering these inner obstacles, providing valuable insights, strategies, and inspiration to empower you in your journey of self-discovery, resilience, and success. It's time to break free from the shackles of self-doubt and unlock the true power that lies within.

What Are Limiting Beliefs?

Do you ever find yourself saying something like, "I am not very creative and not good at artistic endeavors," or "I have terrible balance and can't ski?" I know I have!! Those are two of my own limiting beliefs.

Limiting beliefs are deeply ingrained thoughts, ideas, or perceptions that hold individuals back from realizing their full potential or pursuing their goals. These beliefs are often negative, self-defeating, and based on subjective interpretations rather than objective reality. Limiting beliefs act as mental barriers, constraining individuals from taking action, embracing opportunities, or reaching their desired outcomes. They are stories you may tell yourself that you believe to be true that limit you. They're false beliefs that prevent you from pursuing your goals and dreams. They hold you back from being who you want to become. It's a restrictive state of mind that you create. Your inner voice tells you you're not good enough and questions your abilities, skills, talent, and courage.

Examples of Common Limiting Beliefs

"I'm too old." Or "I'm too young."
." I'm not smart enough."
"I don't have enough experience."
"I don't have enough time." Or "I don't have enough money."
"I am not a leader."

"That's not something I'm good at."
"I am not good at numbers."
"I'm not very creative."
"I am not attractive enough."
"I am not good at meeting people."
"I can't do that."

How do limiting beliefs affect lawyers?

What are some of your most problematic limiting beliefs? These beliefs, deeply rooted in your mindset, can hinder your personal and professional growth. Some of the most prevalent limiting beliefs for lawyers include:

"I'm not good enough."

Many lawyers struggle with a persistent feeling of inadequacy, doubting their abilities and fearing that they don't meet their colleagues' or clients' expectations.

"Success requires sacrifice."

Lawyers may believe they must sacrifice their personal lives and well-being to achieve professional success. Unfortunately, this belief can lead to burnout and an imbalance between work and personal life.

"Mistakes are unforgivable."

Due to the high-stakes nature of their profession, lawyers often fear making mistakes, viewing them as catastrophic failures rather than learning opportunities. This fear can stifle innovation and growth.

"I have to know everything."

Lawyers may feel immense pressure to have all the answers and be experts in every aspect of the law. Unfortunately, this belief can create anxiety and prevent them from seeking help or collaborating with others.

"Work defines my worth."
Lawyers often tie their self-worth solely to their professional achievements, neglecting other aspects of their identity and well-being.

"Taking risks is dangerous."
Fear of failure and the potential consequences can deter lawyers from taking calculated risks, often necessary for professional advancement and innovation.

These limiting beliefs are not based on objective truths but somewhat subjective perceptions that can be challenged and overcome with self-awareness, support, and a growth-oriented mindset.

What Causes Limiting Beliefs?

Now that you know what limiting beliefs are, where do they come from? What causes them? Some come from family upbringing and the beliefs instilled in your mind. Some come from your educational background. Persons and places of authority may have planted specific ideas that you have about yourself. Others come from personal experiences. These all progressively evolve and change, developing into your limiting beliefs.

Most importantly, your limiting beliefs are self-created. They come from your brain's desire to protect you from suffering pain in the future. Whether due to fear or imposter syndrome, limiting beliefs come from the inside and stop you from feeling unsuccessful. They tell you not to try something you could be good at so you don't feel like a failure if it doesn't work out. You retain your limiting beliefs to protect yourself from struggles and failures.

What Causes Limiting Beliefs For Lawyers?

Understanding these causes can illuminate the origins of limiting beliefs within the legal profession. Here are some of the most significant reasons:

Perfectionism and High Standards

Pursuing perfection and the high standards prevalent in the legal field can pressure lawyers immensely. The fear of making mistakes or falling short of expectations can lead to the development of limiting beliefs, such as the belief that anything less than perfection is unacceptable.

Law School and Legal Culture

Law school is challenging, and law is a very competitive field. The rigorous nature of legal education and the competitive culture within the profession can foster a mindset of self-doubt and comparison. The emphasis on intellectual prowess and the constant need to prove oneself can contribute to the formation of limiting beliefs about one's abilities and worthiness.

Adverse Experiences

You may lose a case, a client may leave for another firm, or the partner may criticize you. Then, you can begin to think you're not good enough. Negative experiences can impact your mindset. These experiences can reinforce limiting beliefs, making them more deeply ingrained and difficult to overcome.

Comparison and Imposter Syndrome

Lawyers often compare themselves to their peers, colleagues, or high-profile individuals in the legal field. This constant comparison can fuel imposter syndrome, where lawyers feel they are not as competent or deserving of their success as others, leading to limiting beliefs about their capabilities.

Lack of Mentoring and Support Systems

Mentoring is critical to developing your skill set as a lawyer. Sadly, young lawyers often do not receive the coaching they need. A lack of mentors who have successfully navigated similar challenges can contribute to the development of limiting beliefs. Lawyers may need guidance or support systems to challenge their assumptions and find alternative perspectives.

Negative Self-Talk

Lawyers may engage in negative self-talk, continuously criticizing themselves or discounting their accomplishments. This negative internal dialogue reinforces limiting beliefs and undermines self-confidence.

Fear of Taking Risks

What if you take that chance and fail? The legal profession is often risk-averse due to the potential consequences of errors or ethical breaches. This emphasis on risk mitigation can lead lawyers to develop limiting beliefs about taking calculated risks and pursuing new opportunities.

Workload and Stress

So many lawyers are overwhelmed by their daunting workload. The demanding nature of legal work, long hours, and high-stakes cases can contribute to stress and burnout. The resulting mental and emotional exhaustion can make lawyers more susceptible to adopting limiting beliefs.

Our experiences are unique, so this is only a partial list. But many of us have experienced some of these. By identifying the causes and understanding their influence, you can begin to challenge and overcome your limiting beliefs, ultimately fostering a more empowering and fulfilling professional journey. Because limiting beliefs come from your experiences and history and are mainly self-created, you can manage and control them.

How Do Limiting Beliefs Affect You?

What is the effect of these limiting beliefs? Limiting beliefs harm your development, growth, and success. We fail to achieve your dreams. You're unhappy and unfulfilled. Who wants THAT??!!

Some of the ways they can affect you:

Self-Doubt

Am I capable? Can I do this? Limiting beliefs erode lawyers' self-confidence, leading to self-doubt and diminished confidence in their abilities. This self-doubt hinders your performance.

Impaired Decision-Making

You begin to question yourself. Are you right? What should you do next? Lawyers with limiting beliefs may second-guess themselves excessively, leading to analysis paralysis and difficulty making confident decisions. This can slow progress, impact case outcomes, and limit your ability to provide effective counsel, leading to a self-fulfilling prophecy.

Fear of Failure

What if it doesn't work out right? Limiting beliefs often instill a fear of failure in lawyers. They don't want to fail and are often afraid of that result. That causes risk aversion, avoiding opportunities leading to growth and success. This fear can prevent you from taking on challenging cases or pursuing career advancements.

Professional Stagnation

When lawyers hold onto limiting beliefs, they may resist stepping outside their comfort zones and embracing new opportunities for growth and advancement. This stagnation causes a lack of professional development and hinders your ability to reach your full potential.

Burnout and Work-Life Imbalance

Lawyers who believe success requires sacrificing their personal lives may experience burnout and struggle to maintain a healthy work-life balance. This lack of balance can lead to chronic stress, diminished well-being, and strained relationships.

Limited Networking

Limiting beliefs can hinder lawyers' willingness to network and collaborate with others. You're afraid to meet people or won't be able to connect. Avoiding networking can limit your access to mentorship, peer support, and valuable professional connections, inhibiting your professional growth and opportunities for collaboration.

Addressing and overcoming limiting beliefs is crucial for thriving in your career, enhancing your well-being, and maximizing your impact in the legal profession. By challenging these beliefs and cultivating a growth mindset, you can unlock your full potential and overcome these challenges.

Tools For Overcoming Limiting Beliefs

We want to avoid passing up experiences that could help us succeed. We want to take advantage of opportunities that could help us achieve our dreams. How do you overcome your limiting beliefs?

Identify Your Limiting Beliefs

Developing self-awareness is the first step in identifying and understanding limiting beliefs. Write down your thoughts, good and evil, and everything you believe to be true. Focus on any ideas you feel strongly about that influence you daily. Writing them down will allow you to understand each one and reflect on its validity.

Question Your Beliefs

Examine those beliefs you wrote down. Assess the accuracy of each one. Consider whether each is true. The belief loses its power once you understand it may not be valid. Ask yourself, "What if I am wrong?" What would my world look like if this belief were not true? Is there any concrete evidence to support this belief? Does it come from a place of fear or your experience? Imagine your life if that belief were not true. Understand that your beliefs are not your truth.

Determine if the Belief Serves You

These are the critical questions: Does this belief help you grow? Does that belief help you to be successful or hold you back? If the idea doesn't serve you, is it worthwhile holding onto?

Disprove the Belief

Look for evidence contradicting the belief. Is it the absolute truth? Or is it a lie you tell yourself to protect yourself?

Create Alternative Beliefs

Change any belief that limits you. Are there contrary or different beliefs that may also be true? A more helpful view that serves you better? Look for other options. For example, I wondered if I was too mature to begin my podcast, The Free Lawyer. Instead of saying, "I am too old to start a podcast," I can tell myself, "I have a lot of experience I can share with others." Reframe those unhelpful beliefs. Be creative. Write down alternative hypotheses to your limiting one that may also be true and more helpful to you.

Obtain Support

Lawyers can benefit from guidance from mentors who provide objective perspectives, encouragement, and accountability. Connecting with others overcoming similar limiting beliefs can be affirming. Talk to someone about your limiting beliefs. Explain what they are. Your mentor can help you see that they simply are stories you tell yourself that limit your success.

Empower Yourself to Choose a Different Belief

Limiting beliefs do not serve you. They don't help you accomplish your goals. It's time to throw them in the garbage. Choose the alternative view. Use your power to select one that allows you to be your best self.

Visualize a Successful Result

Use visualization techniques to rehearse success and envision yourself overcoming challenges mentally. You can reinforce a more empowering belief system by vividly imagining positive outcomes and embodying the emotions associated with those achievements.

By combining these tools and approaches, you can gradually dismantle limiting beliefs and cultivate a more empowered mindset that fosters personal and professional growth.

Conclusion

Overcoming your limiting beliefs becomes imperative for unleashing your true potential. Determining which of your ingrained beliefs are worth holding on to helps you live the life you've always dreamed of. When you change your perspective, you can change your life.

By recognizing and dismantling self-imposed barriers, you liberate yourself from self-doubt, propel your career forward, and catalyze positive change in the entire legal realm. The path to overcoming limiting beliefs may not always be easy, but It's worthwhile.

You deserve to be free of these limiting beliefs and to be as fulfilled and happy as you want.

Section 2
Keys to Freedom

Key 1: Acceptance

(EMBRACING ACCEPTANCE: THE LAWYER'S PATH TO FREEDOM)

"Acceptance doesn't mean resignation; it means understanding that something is what it is and that there's got to be a way through it."
– Michael J. Fox

Do you ever feel overwhelmed and don't know how to achieve peace in the chaos?

Are you stressed by your workload or by your partner or other attorneys and stuck ruminating about them?

Are you frustrated that you cannot control events in your life?

Practicing acceptance can be a transformative and empowering mindset for those working in the law field. The path of acceptance invites you to navigate your challenges with grace, resilience, and inner peace. By embracing acceptance, you can liberate yourself from the burdens of perfectionism, resistance to change, and the constant need for control.

It offers a powerful tool to navigate the complexities of this profession while fostering personal well-being, improving client relationships, and enhancing the overall effectiveness of your practice. This chapter examines the profound benefits of practicing acceptance as a lawyer. Explore practical strategies, real-life experiences, and insights to guide you on this transformative journey of acceptance.

What Does It Mean To Practice Acceptance?

Acceptance is acknowledging and embracing reality as it is without judgment or resistance. It involves recognizing and allowing things to be pleasant or unpleasant without trying to change or control them. Acceptance is a mindset that promotes inner peace, resilience, and emotional well-being.

Practicing acceptance doesn't mean resignation or passivity. It's not about giving up or surrendering to unfavorable situations. Instead, It's a conscious choice to let go of resistance and emotional struggle, understanding that some things are beyond your control. It's about shifting your focus from what you cannot change to what you can, such as your reactions, attitudes, and choices. Acceptance requires self-awareness, mindfulness, and a willingness to embrace reality with an open heart and mind.

Acceptance invites you to make peace with your past, be present in the current moment, and face the future with equanimity. You stop reacting to and judging yourself, others, and the circumstances of life. By embracing acceptance, you can reduce stress, anxiety, and suffering. It allows you to navigate life's challenges with greater ease, wisdom, and inner strength.

Why Do You Need To Practice Acceptance?

Often, the law profession itself causes incredible stress. Your senior partner may be demanding to work with, not listening to you, and barking orders. Your clients may ignore your advice, calling you incessantly and voicing frustrations. Then there are the time pressures, which can become overwhelming, and there's always more work piling up.

At times, that stress goes home with you. Add to the fact that there may be problems at home: finances, your children struggling with school, or your relationship's strained. Much of it can be beyond your control. You may feel powerless, with little you can do, increasing your stress. How do you find serenity in the midst of all of this anxiety and pressure?

The Practice of Acceptance

One beneficial solution is to practice acceptance. By now, most have heard of the Serenity Prayer:

> *"God grant me the serenity to accept the things I cannot change; the courage to change the things I can; and the wisdom to know the difference."*

This simple prayer holds the key to finding serenity in your daily life amidst all the storms you face. You have little power over so much in your life. Yet, you resist each of those things. You battle with them. You try to swim against the powerful tide. That only increases your frustration and your stress. The key word in that prayer is "accept." That tiny word holds tremendous power.

What do you do with the many circumstances and people in your life that you can't change or control? You learn to accept each completely, as being what It's supposed to be, without judging. If you learn to accept circumstances without fighting, getting mad, or trying to change them into something they aren't, you free yourself from stress. You release yourself from the adverse reactions you might create. With all the many pressures you face, you generate emotional stress when you resist them. You let that circumstance or other person control your emotions and happiness.

Instead of fighting those circumstances, you can accept it as the reality you face. Do not judge it. Do not fight it. You do not take harmful behaviors from others or feel hopeless, but empower yourself to let go of the anger and blame you might feel. Instead of creating stress about the circumstances, simply say, "It is what it is."

Acceptance is the answer to all your frustrations today. When stressed, you find some person or situation unacceptable. When you stop living in the problem and begin living in the solution, you free yourself from self-inflicted frustrations. You can become thrilled when you accept life completely on life's terms. You feel more serene when you focus on what needs to be changed in yourself and your attitudes instead of what you want to change "out there."

When you're not accepting, you're allowing yourself to be deeply troubled by a person or circumstance, which takes away serenity. Acceptance helps you to understand that you can't change some things. But you can accept how that makes you feel, even if you do not like it. Ultimately, you learn to accept it even though it makes you uncomfortable. It still is what it is.

Is acceptance easy? Of course not. It takes practice. But, whenever you're frustrated by someone or circumstance in your life, try to understand that you don't have the power to change them, but you have control over your response and attitudes.

The Biggest Obstacles To Practicing Acceptance

If acceptance is so beneficial, why don't you all do it all the time?? These are some of the obstacles to practicing acceptance:

Resistance to Change

Change is difficult! Humans naturally resist change, especially when it challenges existing beliefs, habits, or comfort zones. Accepting a situation often requires letting go of familiar patterns and embracing the unknown, which can trigger resistance.

Ego and Attachment

Egos seek validation, control, and identity. It can lead you to attach to specific outcomes. Letting go of these attachments and accepting things as they are can be a struggle as it challenges the ego's need for certainty and control.

Overthinking
The mind overanalyzes, constantly questioning and replaying past events and worrying about the future. This overthinking can create resistance to accepting the present moment and hinder the practice of acceptance.

Emotional Avoidance
Unpleasant emotions, such as sadness, fear, or anger, can be uncomfortable to experience. You may suppress these emotions, which can prevent the practice of acceptance. Accepting feelings as they arise and absorbing them without judgment is essential to acceptance.

Lack of Self-Awareness
It can be challenging to recognize your resistance. You're likely unaware of your resistance patterns, making it difficult to practice acceptance consciously.

Overcoming these obstacles requires patience, self-compassion, and a willingness to cultivate awareness and make conscious choices.

What Are The Gifts Of Acceptance?

Acceptance allows you to find serenity in your life by creating calm and peacefulness and removing your emotional adverse reaction to your immediate troubles.

When you practice acceptance, you transform your life and attitude:

- You free yourself from the unhealthy expectations of others.
- You experience less stress and worry.
- You stop trying to control people.
- You enjoy greater freedom, humility, and hope.

- You find greater strength and courage to live as you want.
- You open your life to greater possibilities and visions for success.

When you practice acceptance, your focus changes from people and circumstances you cannot control to what you can change, yourself. Most importantly, acceptance frees you from an unhealthy compulsion to control others and their circumstances. When you try to control, you're constantly frustrated because you don't have the power to change other people. You can choose to accept without judgment.

How Can Lawyers Benefit From Practicing Acceptance?

You may ask yourself, "Acceptance sounds like a great concept for some people, but how can it help me in my legal practice?" The gifts of acceptance to you as a lawyer are profound. Here are just a few:

Reduced Stress and Burnout

Law practice can be demanding, and lawyers often face high pressure. Acceptance helps to let go of perfectionism, unrealistic expectations, and the need to control every outcome. By accepting the circumstances and unpredictability of the profession, you can reduce stress and prevent burnout.

Improved Decision-Making

Acceptance allows lawyers to approach their cases and legal issues with a clear and focused mind. By accepting the facts and circumstances as they are, without any resistance, you can make more objective and rational decisions without bias, leading to better outcomes for your clients.

Enhanced Resilience

The legal profession can be challenging, with setbacks and disappointments. Practicing acceptance enables you to bounce back from adversities more effectively. You can learn from failures, adapt to unexpected situations, and maintain a resilient attitude when facing challenges.

Improved Client Relationships

Acceptance helps lawyers approach their clients with empathy, understanding, and non-judgment. By accepting your clients' perspectives, emotions, and needs, you can build stronger trust and rapport, leading to more effective communication and better client outcomes.

Better Conflict Resolution

Acceptance fosters a more constructive approach to conflict resolution. Lawyers can approach negotiations, mediations, and disputes more openly and flexibly. You can listen attentively, understand different viewpoints, and work towards finding mutually beneficial solutions.

Increased Self-Awareness

Practicing acceptance involves self-reflection. Lawyers who cultivate acceptance can better understand their strengths, limitations, biases, and emotional triggers. This self-awareness can help make conscious choices, manage emotions, and interact more effectively with clients, colleagues, and judges.

Improved Work-Life Balance

Acceptance allows lawyers to balance their professional and personal lives. By accepting that work will never be perfect or finished, lawyers can set realistic boundaries and prioritize self-care. This balance improves your well-being, satisfaction, and overall quality of life.

Enhanced Professional Relationships

Acceptance extends to interactions with colleagues, opposing counsel, and the court. Lawyers who practice acceptance can build more collaborative relationships within the legal profession. These better relationships lead to better teamwork, more effective advocacy, and improved outcomes for your clients.

By incorporating acceptance into your daily life and legal practices, you'll experience many benefits, promoting your well-being, effectiveness, and professional success.

What Are The 10 Steps To Practicing Acceptance In Your Daily Lives?

Practicing acceptance in your life can bring significant positive changes. Here are ten steps to cultivating a practice of acceptance:

1. **Mindfulness:**
   Develop a mindful awareness of your thoughts and emotions in the present moment. Observe them without judgment or resistance, allowing them to come and go naturally.

2. **Letting go of control:**
   Recognize that aspects of life are beyond your control. Instead of trying to manipulate them, focus on what you can control—your attitudes, actions, and responses.

3. **Self-compassion:**
   Treat yourself with kindness and understanding. Embrace your flaws, imperfections, and past mistakes. Practice self-forgiveness and let go of self-criticism.

4. **Embracing change:**
   Understand that everything in life is transient. Accept that change is inevitable, and learn to adapt and flow with the natural rhythm of life.

5. **Non-judgment:**
   Challenge your tendency to label experiences as good or bad. Instead, cultivate an attitude of curiosity and openness, exploring the lessons and opportunities present in each situation.

6. **Gratitude:**
   Cultivate a sense of appreciation for what you have, even amidst difficulties. Recognize the positive aspects of your life and express gratitude regularly.

7. **Reframing perspectives:**
   Practice reframing negative situations by looking for alternative viewpoints or silver linings. Seek lessons or growth opportunities in challenging experiences.

8. **Emotional resilience:**
   Develop the capacity to tolerate discomfort and uncertainty. Allow yourself to fully feel emotions without avoiding or suppressing them, knowing they will pass in time.

9. **Practice acceptance with others:**
   Extend acceptance to the people in your life. Recognize that everyone has their own journey and experience. Foster empathy and understanding toward others' perspectives and behaviors.

10. **Seek support:**
    If acceptance feels challenging, consider seeking help from friends, family, your mentor, or a therapist. They can provide guidance, perspective, and encouragement on your journey.

Remember that practicing acceptance is a gradual process that requires patience and self-compassion. But integrating these practices into your daily life allows you to develop a greater sense of peace, resilience, and well-being.

Conclusion

Acceptance is not a sign of weakness but a testament to strength, wisdom, and growth. By cultivating acceptance, lawyers can transcend the limitations of ego, embrace the realities of their profession, and tap into their true potential as compassionate advocates for their clients.

As you embark on your journey of acceptance, may you find the courage to let go of what cannot be changed, the resilience to face challenges with grace, and the profound peace that comes from aligning with the flow of life. Embrace acceptance as a guiding principle, and watch as it transforms your practice and your entire approach to the law and the world around you.

Key 2: Gratitude

"I am happy because I'm grateful. I choose to be grateful. That gratitude allows me to be happy."
–Will Arnett

Have you ever felt overwhelmed by stress?

Do you have days you feel that simply nothing goes right?

Do you see others who appear so happy and wish you felt like that?

One critical tool in overcoming those feelings is having a practice of gratitude. Cultivating gratitude can be a transformative and invaluable tool for lawyers. Incorporating gratitude into your professional lives enhances well-being, improves mental health, reduces stress, strengthens relationships, and fosters a positive outlook.

By expressing appreciation for the positive aspects of your work, acknowledging the support received, and recognizing the opportunities within your profession, you can experience increased job satisfaction, resilience, and a more profound sense of purpose. In this chapter, you'll learn about gratitude and how to avoid the obstacles to practicing gratitude in your profession. And you'll get the steps to create a gratitude practice that frees you from stress.

What Is Gratitude?

Gratitude is the feeling of being thankful, appreciative, and acknowledging the kindness, help, and benefits received from others. It's when you actively recognize and show a grateful spirit for the positive aspects of life, including the people, experiences, and opportunities that contribute to your well-being and happiness.

Expressing gratitude involves more than just saying "thank you." It means genuine appreciation and recognition of the value that you've received. You can express gratitude toward individuals, such as friends, family members, mentors, or even strangers who have shown kindness, and toward intangible aspects of life, such as nature, good health, personal accomplishments, or opportunities that come your way.

What Obstacles Do Lawyers Face When Attempting To Practice Gratitude?

Attorneys face many competing pressures and tensions that can interfere with your gratitude. Here are some:

Time Pressures
Lawyers have such demanding schedules with billable hour requirements, multiple cases, client meetings, court appearances, and deadlines to manage. Those pressures can interfere with the ability to feel grateful.

High-Stress Environment
Practicing law leads to many high-pressure situations, demanding workloads, and long hours, which makes it challenging to find the time and mental space for gratitude practices.

Negative Outlook
The adversarial nature of legal proceedings and the constant

conflicts can lead to a more cynical mindset, making it harder to adopt a gratitude practice.

Perfectionism and High Expectations

Many lawyers struggle with perfectionism. Personal expectations often create stress. The legal profession encourages a perfectionistic mindset, focusing on what needs to be improved or corrected. This mindset can make it difficult to shift focus towards gratitude and appreciating what is already present.

Emotional Toll

Attorneys frequently have to handle emotionally charged situations, traumatic events, and intense courtroom battles. These situations affect emotional well-being, making having and showing gratitude more difficult.

Competitive Environment

Attorneys face competition every day. Contests with other lawyers and competition for business inside and outside your firm are everyday experiences. Competition fosters a sense of comparison and rivalry and may create a mindset focused on achievement and success rather than gratitude and appreciation.

Lack of Awareness

Do you struggle with being mindful and truly present under all these pressures? If so, you may need to understand your current feelings and how to refocus them on gratitude. Overcoming these obstacles requires conscious effort and a commitment to prioritizing gratitude.

But it's so worth the effort!

What Are The Gifts Of Gratitude?

When you're not grateful, you might feel as if you're full of self-centered fear, stress, and anxiety. You may feel sorry for yourself as if you're not getting what you're entitled to. It leads to always wanting more and becoming afraid of losing what you have. Essentially, you're depressed, even miserable.

How does having an attitude of gratitude help? Here are some of the many gifts of gratitude:

Joy

When you feel grateful, you have a true sensation of happiness. You can see how you're blessed. You appreciate your gifts and feel profound joy. Who doesn't want to feel happier?

Less Stress

Practicing law is stressful. However, gratitude practices can help you manage stress more effectively. Expressing gratitude can reduce anxiety, improve resilience, and promote a sense of calm amidst challenges. When you practice gratitude, your emotions are better balanced, and you feel a sense of calm. If things seem overwhelming, being grateful for the many gifts in your life can help you maintain a better perspective. You'll see that what bothers you is not that important, given all you have to be grateful for.

Better Sleep

If you feel grateful when you go to bed at night, you'll sleep better. Being stressed and overwhelmed is a recipe for a restless night, but when your mind is clear and thinking only positive thoughts, you'll enjoy a better and longer night's sleep.

Improved Relationships

Expressing gratitude towards colleagues and clients strengthens professional relationships. Appreciation fosters a sense of connection, trust, and mutual respect, leading to more positive interactions, improved teamwork, and a supportive work environment. In your personal life, those relationships improve when you practice gratitude. We all enjoy being around someone who is expressing appreciation. When you're grateful, you're more calm and empathetic, less aggressive, and less angry. That supports our relationships with friends and family.

Self-Esteem

Gratitude can increase your self-esteem. When you're thankful for your gifts, you feel better about yourself. You stop comparing yourself to others and begin to reflect on what you have, which always makes you feel better. You end up appreciating those around you more.

Resilience

Grateful people are more resilient. Gratitude practices enhance your resilience by helping you to reframe challenges. By focusing on what you're thankful for, you develop a more optimistic perspective, bounce back from setbacks more efficiently, and maintain motivation in the face of adversity. When you feel sorry for yourself, thinking of what you do not have, the least little obstacle sets you back. But when you're thankful for the many gifts in your lives, you have a different outlook on the hurdles you face. You respond to hurdles better.

Generosity

You're much more willing to share your time, money, or talents when you realize how blessed you are. By contrast, generosity becomes your last emotion when you feel you're a victim and stressed. So, gratitude helps you to become more generous.

Optimism

When you're grateful, you tend to focus more on your blessings. You're thankful for the people and circumstances in your life. And that creates hope for the future when the glass appears half full.

Purpose

On days when you feel thankful for being able to help others, you're grateful to be of service. You appreciate your talents and experience that allow you to improve the lives of others. Your work obtains a more significant meaning, and you feel purpose in what you're doing.

Improved Client Relationships

Expressing your gratitude towards clients can deepen the attorney-client relationship. Clients who feel appreciated are likelier to trust their lawyers, leading to better communication, collaboration, and client satisfaction.

Enhanced Job Satisfaction

Gratitude practices can help lawyers find greater meaning and purpose in their work. Recognizing the positive impact on others' lives, appreciating your accomplishments, and acknowledging new opportunities can increase job satisfaction and motivation.

Better Work-Life Balance

Gratitude helps lawyers shift their focus from work-related stressors to the positive aspects of their personal lives. This contributes to a healthier work-life balance, improving overall well-being and satisfaction.

How to Practice Gratitude

Those are some incredible gifts for feeling more grateful. But when you're in a place where negativity overwhelms you, how can you create that powerful gratitude that can lift you? Here are some steps:

Reflect on the Positive

Take a few moments each day to reflect on the positive aspects of your work as a lawyer. Consider the cases you have successfully handled, the clients you have helped, or the skills you have developed. Acknowledge the achievements and progress you have made.

Be Mindful

Incorporate mindfulness into your daily routine to help you stay present and focus on the positive aspects of your work. Engage in mindful breathing exercises or take short mindful breaks throughout the day to center yourself and cultivate a sense of gratitude. Be aware of the little things that happen each day for which you are grateful. You'll be amazed how often, each day, some positive events occur. When you're conscious of each moment in your day and are thankful for each little circumstance that worked out positively, you'll feel much more grateful.

Express Appreciation

Be grateful to colleagues, clients, or mentors who've positively impacted your legal career. Send a thank-you note, have a genuine conversation expressing your appreciation, or publicly acknowledge their contributions. Small acts of gratitude can go a long way in fostering positive relationships. When you feel thankful for someone in your life, let them know. Tell them how much you appreciate who they are and what they do. Express to them that you're grateful for how they have supported you. You'll internally feel more appreciative when you express your gratitude to others.

Serve Others

While you may face difficulties, many are even less fortunate. Look for opportunities to help others. Be a mentor to a young person in need; help in your church or rec council; volunteer to serve food to the homeless; or find another avenue that suits your desires to volunteer. When you're of service, you realize that no matter how many things in your life are not what you want them to be, you are, in many ways, very blessed.

Try Daily Journaling

Make it a daily practice to set aside a few minutes each day to write down three things you're thankful for in your professional life. It could be a supportive colleague, a positive outcome in a case, or even the opportunity to make a difference in someone's life.

Writing them down reinforces your appreciation and helps cultivate a gratitude mindset. Start tomorrow by recording three *new* circumstances in your life for which you're grateful, and do this for 30 days. After the first few days, you might need to reflect on your life and search more deeply to ascertain already unstated items, but it's worth it. At the end of the 30 days, you'll have recorded at least 90 different items. Then, end your day by reviewing your list before you go to bed. Beginning and ending your day with the things you're grateful for gives you more resilience during the day and a better night's sleep.

Find Gratitude in Challenges

When facing challenging situations, try to find something to be grateful for. It could be an opportunity for personal growth, the chance to develop resilience, or the lessons learned from the experience. Shifting your perspective can help you navigate challenges with a more positive mindset.

Create Gratitude Rituals

Establish regular rituals that remind you to practice gratitude. For example, start or end each day by sharing one thing you're grateful for with a colleague or incorporate gratitude exercises into team meetings or client interactions. Making gratitude part of your routine becomes a habit that strengthens over time.

Seek Support

Connect with other lawyers interested in practicing gratitude or join professional networks or organizations that promote well-being in the legal field. A supportive mentor can help you appreciate what you must be grateful for.

Remember, incorporating gratitude into your professional life is a gradual process. Start with small steps and be consistent. Over time, practicing gratitude can transform your outlook, well-being, and overall satisfaction as a lawyer.

Conclusion

The practice of gratitude holds immense power for lawyers, offering a profound shift in perspective and enhancing your professional life. By embracing gratitude, lawyers can navigate the profession's challenges with resilience, find joy and fulfillment in the work, and cultivate stronger relationships with colleagues and clients. Expressing appreciation and recognizing the positive aspects of the legal journey can lead to increased job satisfaction, improved mental well-being, and a greater sense of purpose.

By implementing the practical steps listed above, you enjoy a transformative journey toward a more fulfilling professional life. Gratitude can be the guiding force that shapes your legal career and fosters a deep appreciation for the privilege of practicing law.

Key 3: Living in the Present

(SUCCESSFUL LAWYERING: THE POWER OF
LIVING IN THE PRESENT)

*"If you want to be happy, do not dwell in the past, do not
worry about the future, focus on living fully in the present."*
–Roy Bennett

**Do you ever find you're distracted, worrying
about the future and how things will turn out?**

**Do you worry about what other people might
be thinking of you?**

**Do you ever resent what people have done to
you in the past?**

**How often do you find yourself thinking
about what happened yesterday or what might
happen tomorrow?**

How does that make you feel?

One of the biggest challenges in creating personal fulfillment is living in the present and avoiding the past or future ensnaring us. Unfortunately, both of those create obstacles to your attaining personal freedom.

Living in the present is an elusive luxury in a stressful world. So often, humans waste precious energy thinking about past events, how others hurt them, or even what they might have done wrong. Too frequently, obsessing about the future and imagining poor outcomes takes up head space.

However, pause for a moment and consider this: What if the key to legal success and personal well-being lies in the art of being fully present? Intentionally immersing oneself in the here and now can serve as a transformative tool in a profession marked by its demanding nature. This chapter explores why and how lawyers should embrace the power of the present moment. Discover how this can help you to become a better lawyer and ultimately pave the way to a more fulfilling legal career.

What Does It Mean to Live in the Present?

Living in the present means focusing your attention and awareness on the current moment without getting caught up in regrets about the past or worries about the future. It involves fully immersing yourself in your actions, thinking, and experiences. Here are a few critical aspects of living in the present:

Awareness of the Moment

Self-awareness involves paying attention to your thoughts, emotions, sensations, and surroundings as they happen in the present. Instead of letting your mind wander, you intentionally focus on the here and now.

Letting Go of Distractions

Living in the present means acknowledging distractions and letting them pass without attaching too much importance to them. This helps you stay centered on what you're engaged in.

Mindful Activities

Engaging in tasks mindfully involves doing them with full attention. For example, savor each bite and notice the flavors, textures, and smells when eating. When walking, pay attention to each step and the sensations in your body.

Acceptance and Non-Judgment

Living in the present involves accepting things without harsh judgment. Accept your emotions and thoughts without suppressing or overly dwelling on them.

What Are Some Gifts Of The Present?

The past is full of disappointment, regret, and resentment. The future creates stress, worry, and anxiety. But the present is a true gift. Being truly present, enjoying one moment at a time, and being mindful helps to create an amazingly fulfilling life. Here are ten incredible gifts of living in the present:

Self-Control

Being in the present is the only time you can control your attitudes, responses, and behaviors. You decide what day you want to have and what kind of experience you want to enjoy. You can choose to be happy.

Truly Feel Peace

Even in stressful times, when you're present in the moment, accepting what is, and being as present as possible with those around you, you can truly experience peace. The negative feelings of the past and future cannot disturb the peacefulness of living in the present.

Enjoy Every Moment

Life presents itself as individual experiences. Therefore, you can live and appreciate every one of them as they occur.

Acceptance

When you let go of what should be, you can accept what is. You'll free yourself of the comparison and expectation which lead to resentment and disappointment. Instead, you'll appreciate your life as it is.

Experience gratitude

You'll be more grateful for everything: the sunrise, time with your puppies, and the touch of your spouse's hand, to name a few.

Truly Experience Life

Life will slow down when you focus on being present in the moment.

Improved Relationships

When you sincerely focus, listen purposefully, and are genuinely present with your friends and loved ones, you'll have better communication and more positive relationships.

More Happiness

We will be happier, enjoying each moment, fulfilled, and not burdened by the negative emotions of the past or future.

More Productivity

When focused at work and intent on what you're doing, you'll be more successful in your profession and of better service to others.

Reach Your Dreams

You can finally make the changes you dreamed of. Your goals start with the steps you take today. Now is the time for change.

Why Is It Essential For A Lawyer To Live In The Present?

Living in the present directly impacts professional effectiveness and well-being. Here's why:

Focused Client Interaction

Lawyers must understand their clients' concerns, needs, and perspectives. Being fully present during client meetings means listening actively, asking relevant questions, and offering meaningful advice.

This fosters trust and enhances the attorney-client relationship.

Effective Communication

Clear and concise communication is vital in the legal profession. Being present during discussions, negotiations, and courtroom proceedings enables you to articulate your points effectively, respond to opposing arguments, and convey your clients' interests persuasively.

Attentive Case Handling

Attorney matters involve intricate details and timelines. You can better manage cases, stay organized, and make well-informed decisions by being present.

Critical Thinking and Problem-Solving

You face complex legal issues that require sharp analytical skills. Staying present allows you to fully engage with the details of a case, assess various options, and devise creative solutions to challenges.

Minimizing Mistakes

Legal work demands precision. Mistakes can have serious consequences for clients. Living in the present helps you avoid errors due to lack of attention, ultimately safeguarding your client's interests.

Reducing Stress and Burnout

The legal profession can be highly demanding and stressful. Focusing on the present moment helps manage stress by preventing the accumulation of worries about past cases or future challenges. This can lead to improved mental well-being and job satisfaction.

Enhancing Decision-Making

Lawyers must make rapid decisions in courtrooms, negotiations, and other contexts. Being present allows us to evaluate the situation without being influenced by irrelevant factors or past experiences, leading to more informed choices.

Building Credibility

You establish a reputation for professionalism when you're engaged and respectful in your interactions. This reputation can positively impact your standing within the legal community and with clients.

Adapting to Changes

Legal proceedings can take unexpected turns. Adaptable lawyers can respond effectively to unforeseen developments, adjusting their real-time strategies to protect client interests.

Work-Life Balance

Many attorneys struggle with work-life balance due to demanding schedules. Being present during work hours makes each moment more efficient, freeing time for personal pursuits and relaxation outside work.

In summary, living in the present is essential to excel in your role, build strong relationships, make informed decisions, and maintain your well-being. By being fully engaged in tasks and interactions, you can navigate the challenges of the legal profession with greater effectiveness and satisfaction.

What Are The Tools For Us To Start Living In The Present?

So, how can you enjoy those fantastic gifts of living in the present? How do you stay out of the past and the future and enjoy the benefits of the present? Here are some tools:

Focus on the Now

Be aware of what you're doing. Be mindful of how you feel. Notice the surroundings around you. Notice all the details. If you're outside, sense the breeze against your face, the sun's warmth, the color of the leaves and grass. Turn off the distractions like the TV or your computer and enjoy the moment. Savor as much as you can of the world around you: the smells, the sights, the sounds, and the feelings. The more mindful you are of your surroundings, the more you appreciate the present.

Smile

Smile often. Smile at strangers. You're in charge of your attitude. Showing warmth to the world around you connects you with the present. Having an attitude of happiness and sharing it with others makes today more enjoyable.

Do Something Nice For Someone For No Reason

Hold the door, offer an umbrella, take soup to a sick friend, carry that older person's groceries, and pay for the order of the person in line behind you. Be spontaneous. Practicing random acts of kindness to those in the world will create a greater appreciation for the present.

Stop Multitasking

The myth of multitasking is only a distraction. Do one thing at a time, with a singular focus, and do it well. If you're speaking to your spouse, eliminate all distractions. If you're playing with your child, make that your only focus. If you're writing a brief, focus only on that. Commit to doing one thing at a time.

Mindful Work Transitions

Before starting a new task, pause to acknowledge the transition. A transition can help you let go of the previous matter and fully engage in the current one.

Active Listening

Practice mindfully listening during conversations. Give your full attention to the speaker without interrupting, and respond thoughtfully after considering what was said.

Nature Walks

Take short walks outside and observe the sights, sounds, and sensations around you. Engaging with nature can help ground you in the present moment.

Journaling

Spend a few minutes daily journaling about your experiences, thoughts, and emotions. This practice encourages self-reflection and awareness.

Stop Worrying

As you practice being mindful, you'll know when your thoughts are drifting to the future, particularly those negative results that concern you. Redirect your thoughts. Realize you have no control over the future. Bring yourself back to the present.

Dream

Dream of the future, but work hard today. You need to have goals and visions of success. But today, focus on steps in your action plan and fulfill that dream.

Be With Friends and Family That Lift You

Surround yourself with those who support you and make you laugh. Avoid the people who are negative and drag you down. Those who love you will help you appreciate the present's gifts.

Bedtime Reflection

Spend a few moments before sleep reflecting on your day. Recognize your accomplishments and acknowledge any challenges, aiming to release any lingering stress.

Forgive

Forgive those who harmed you. Let the wrongs of the past go. It doesn't serve you to worry about what happened in the past.

The wrong was entirely their fault, but allowing it to affect your happiness today is your responsibility.

Accept

Accept those around you for living their life as they choose. Accept circumstances as being precisely what they should be. We have no control over other persons and other circumstances. Resisting them just causes us tension and stress.

Practice Gratitude

Be grateful for your gifts and blessings. Each day, write down the things you have to be thankful for. Being grateful helps you to appreciate the present.

Conclusion

Lawyers are responsible for shaping outcomes that impact lives and society. Embracing living in the present equips you with a profound tool that sharpens your focus, deepens your understanding, and enriches your interactions. Let the power of the present moment illuminate your path forward, allowing you to merge the wisdom of the past with the vitality of the now as you help shape the course of law and life.

Key 4: Forgiveness

(Embracing Forgiveness: A Guide for Lawyers in Conflict)

"Forgiveness is a gift you give yourself, not a gift you give someone else."
–Tony Robbins

Have you ever had someone hurt you
in your life?

Someone who mistreated you unjustifiably
for no good reason?

And you felt, quite justifiably, resentful of how that
person treated you?

Who hasn't been hurt by the actions or
words of another?

And in your law practice, have you been frustrated
with the lawyer who falsely calls you names in court?

Or the judge who makes an entirely erroneous call
against your client?

The partner who is demanding and nasty?

Or the client who fires you unfairly despite your
incredible service?

Emotional wounds can create a reservoir of bitterness, sometimes even vengeance. The key to freeing you from that prison of anger is forgiveness. One of the big problems with permitting yourself to forgive someone else is the misconception about what forgiveness is and isn't.

In the world of law, the concept of forgiveness might seem like an unexpected guest. However, forgiveness holds the potential to be a transformative force, reshaping the dynamics of relationships and fostering a more empathetic approach to advocacy. How often do you pause to explore the profound impact that forgiveness can have on your profession? Keep reading to explore the intersection of forgiveness in the legal world, uncovering how this age-old virtue can guide attorneys to usher in a new era of collaboration, personal growth, and effective conflict resolution.

What is Forgiveness?

Forgiveness is a conscious, deliberate decision to release feelings of resentment toward a person or group that harmed you, regardless of whether they deserve your forgiveness. When you forgive, you stop reliving the pain and feeling over and over again the injury that you suffered. Forgiveness is a purposeful decision to stop holding onto your feelings against another person despite their actions. It releases anger.

When you forgive, you release your bitterness and thoughts of revenge. The "wrong" might always be with you on some level, but forgiveness reduces your pain. It frees you from the control of the person who harmed you. It may even lead to feelings of understanding or compassion for the person who hurt you.

What Does Forgiveness Mean In Your Law Practice?

Forgiveness for lawyers refers to the intentional and conscious act of letting go of negative emotions, resentments, and grudges towards others, including opposing parties, colleagues, clients, the court, and even oneself. It means adopting a compassionate and empathetic perspective, even in conflicts and adversarial situations. Here's what forgiveness means for lawyers:

Release of Negative Emotions

Forgiveness involves releasing anger, resentment, and hostility that may arise from legal disputes or interactions with clients and colleagues. When you consciously choose not to hold onto negative emotions, you move forward more positively and constructively.

Empathy and Understanding

Forgiving requires you to put yourself in the shoes of others, seeking to understand motivations, fears, and concerns. This empathetic approach helps create better communication and conflict resolution.

Acceptance of Imperfection

Forgiveness acknowledges that everyone, including other lawyers, is fallible and prone to mistakes. Lawyers who practice forgiveness recognize that imperfections are part of the human experience and that holding onto blame or judgment may not be productive.

Focus on Positive Outcomes

Forgiveness shifts the focus from past grievances to future possibilities. Lawyers who practice forgiveness are more likely to seek solutions that benefit all parties rather than aiming solely for victory or revenge.

In essence, forgiveness for lawyers is a deliberate choice to approach your legal practice with empathy, compassion, and a focus on favorable resolutions. It empowers you to transcend the adversarial nature of your profession and contribute to a more harmonious career.

What Forgiveness Isn't

Forgiveness is not saying that you're not hurt by what the other person did, didn't feel pain, or that your pain is gone. It also doesn't mean you're not somehow changed by what happened. Forgiveness doesn't excuse the past. It also doesn't mean you're partly to blame for what was done. The old saying "forgive and forget" doesn't reflect the truth; you never have to forget.

Forgiveness doesn't mean condoning what was done to you or even forgetting or excusing the other for the responsibility for the harm they caused. It doesn't mean reconciliation. It doesn't require "making up" with someone who unjustifiably hurt you. You never have to return to the same relationship with that person. It brings you a sense of serenity and frees you from the resentment that entrapped you.

What Are The Hurdles Of Forgiveness?

Sometimes, there are emotional blocks to being able to forgive. Here are some:

Control

Sometimes, you want to control the person who hurt you, make them feel pain, and hold them responsible or accountable. You may think that forgiving lets go of control over the responsibility for what they did.

Expectations

We expect certain behaviors from others, hoping they don't harm unjustifiably. If they do, making proper amends is expected. When they don't do what you wish, the hurt deepens.

Blame

It's natural to blame the other person who harmed you, but that imprisons you. Letting go of blame gives you the power to forgive.

Why You Should Forgive

When you feel a justifiable resentment, you relive the injury. Unfortunately, this re-inflicts the same pain you initially felt, and the experience returns with all the hurt and loss. The only person you hurt when you think that resentment is yourself, no matter how justified your feelings may be. When you forgive, you free yourself from that pain. You're no longer controlled by what the other person did to you.

There are many gifts from forgiveness, such as increased self-esteem, strength, and stability. It allows you to heal and move through life with purpose and intention. You are the primary beneficiary of your forgiveness. It promotes well-being and physical and mental health. The most important thing is that when you forgive the other person, you choose to free yourself from the terrible pain you relive every time you think about how that person harmed you.

The most important gifts of forgiveness include:

Peace
You'll have some measure of serenity and a sense of peace.

Personal Freedom
You're no longer controlled by what that other person did to you. When you need someone else to behave in a certain way, make an apology, or make amends, you're a prisoner to that other person. Forgiveness is about choosing to love yourself and create your freedom.

Healthier Relationships
Forgiveness helps heal your hurt, improve broken relationships, and strengthen your current relationships.

Improved Mental Health
Forgiveness can produce substantial mental health benefits for you. It reduces stress, depression, and anxiety. The negative emotions of blame and hostility are mental burdens. When you release them, you free yourself from the stresses they cause.

Better Physical Health

Those negative emotions strain both emotionally and physically. They affect the heart, immunity, intestinal health, and other physical functions. Forgiveness helps you to be healthier, sleep better, and have more energy.

Forgiveness In Law Practice

Like anyone else, lawyers can benefit significantly from practicing forgiveness personally and professionally. Our profession involves conflict and adversarial situations, so integrating forgiveness into your practice creates several positive outcomes:

Reduced Stress and Burnout

The legal profession is highly stressful, with lawyers frequently dealing with challenging cases and demanding clients. Holding onto negative emotions toward clients or attorneys can contribute to burnout. Forgiveness allows us to release these negative emotions, reducing stress and improving mental well-being.

Improved Relationships

Forgiving others, whether opposing counsel or clients, improves working relationships. Lawyers can foster open communication and collaboration by letting go of grudges, leading to better client outcomes and a more pleasant work atmosphere.

Enhanced Problem Solving

Forgiveness encourages a more empathetic perspective, enabling lawyers to understand the motivations and concerns of others involved in a case. This broader understanding can lead to more effective problem-solving and creative solutions that benefit all parties involved.

Client Trust

Clients are under great stress. Lawyers who practice forgiveness are better equipped to understand their clients' emotions and build trust by offering compassionate and empathetic guidance.

Emotional Resilience

By practicing forgiveness, you develop emotional resilience, which helps you better navigate the profession's ups and downs. This resilience allows you to bounce back from setbacks and perform at your best.

Better Decision-Making

Forgiveness reduces biases and negative emotions that cloud your judgment. Lawyers who practice forgiveness are more likely to make objective and rational decisions, leading to better client outcomes.

Personal Growth

Practicing forgiveness creates personal growth. Lawyers who engage in this practice develop emotional intelligence, empathy, and a deeper understanding of human behavior, all of which contribute to their effectiveness as legal professionals.

Incorporating forgiveness into your law practice requires a shift in mindset. You acknowledge human imperfections and focus on favorable resolutions rather than harboring negative emotions. Forgiveness can help maintain your well-being and strengthen professional relationships.

13 Steps of Forgiving

You can relinquish the resentment once you understand how forgiving helps you create your freedom. You're not condoning wrongdoing but simply releasing yourself from the burden of negative emotions. But it's not always easy. Here are 13 steps you can take to start practicing forgiveness.

1. **Let Go of Judgment**

   A sense of righteousness often holds back from forgiving. You want to judge the other person for their wrongdoing.

But to open yourself to forgiveness, you need to let go of that judgment. Remember, it doesn't condone what he did; it just releases you.

2. **Release Expectations**
Others only sometimes treat us how you want them to. Expectations of other people often do not match their behaviors. When you expect others to behave a certain way, it blocks you from forgiving them. So, let go of your expectations.

3. **Give Up Control**
You can't control the person who harmed you. You can't make them change their behavior, apologize, or make things right. If you try to control what others do and expect an apology, it becomes impossible to move on.

4. **First Forgive Yourself**
Start by not blaming yourself for something you might have done wrong. When you can forgive yourself, you become more able to forgive others.

5. **Understand Your Feelings**
Begin by examining your past experiences. Identify any lingering grudges you might be holding onto. Recognize that forgiveness starts with understanding these emotions. Acknowledge how you feel about what happened and how it affects you. Understanding your emotions is the first step to forgiving the other party and letting go of them.

6. **Shift Perspective**
Try to view the situation from the other person's point of view. Understand their motivations, fears, and challenges. This empathetic perspective can soften your stance and make forgiveness more attainable.

7. **Practice Empathy**
Put yourself in the shoes of the person you're holding a

grudge against. Imagine their emotions and thoughts. This exercise can help you connect with their humanity and see them as more than just adversaries.

8. **Start Small**

Begin with minor instances you find easier to forgive, such as minor misunderstandings. Practice forgiving in these less emotionally charged situations to build your forgiveness muscle.

9. **Open Communication**

If the situation allows, communicate openly and honestly with the person you're forgiving. Sharing your feelings and thoughts can lead to mutual understanding and healing.

10. **Set Boundaries**

Forgiveness doesn't mean allowing harmful behavior to continue. Establishing boundaries to protect yourself from further harm is vital for working towards forgiveness.

11. **Seek Support**

Talk to friends, family, or your mentor about your struggles with forgiveness. Their perspectives can provide valuable insights and encouragement.

12. **Ask for Help with the Willingness to Forgive**

Since forgiveness can be so hard, you need to acquire the desire to let go of your pain. If you're a spiritual person, pray for the willingness to forgive.

13. **Choose to Forgive**

It's not easy, but it's all within your power. To free yourself, choose to forgive the other people who harmed you.

You can free yourself from the other person's control and power when you stop seeing yourself as a victim. Understand that you do not want to give control over your happiness to that very person who harmed you so unjustifiably. Empower yourself by choosing to be free of those burdens.

Conclusion

Forgiveness can be challenging. When you've been unjustifiably wronged, you feel hurt. But reliving that injury causes more pain, doing nothing to the other party. You achieve much greater personal freedom when you choose forgiveness. Lawyers navigate conflicts, disputes, and adversarial situations daily. Forgiveness can transform your approach and elevate the profession. It calls for rising above resentment, seeking understanding amid contention, and forging a path toward healing and resolution.

Embracing forgiveness isn't a sign of weakness; it's a testament to the strength of ethical lawyers, fostering empathy and nurturing the bonds that bind the legal community. Journey forward with an open heart and willingness to let go, knowing that through forgiveness, you empower yourself and shape a profession where compassion and collaboration can thrive.

Key 5: Mindfulness

(From Burnout to Balance: Mindfulness Techniques for Lawyers)

"When we get too caught up in the busyness of the world, we lose connection with one another and ourselves."
– Jack Kornfield

Do you have days where everything gets under your skin and distracts you?

Do you ever get stuck in your head thinking about issues other than the project you're working on?

Or, do you have days where you're laser-focused, not easily rattled, and calmly go about productively solving your clients' problems?

In the world of law, where demands are relentless and stakes are high, the significance of mindfulness cannot be understated. Attorneys must often navigate a maze of stress, burnout, and emotional turbulence. However, embracing mindfulness can unlock a profound source of inner strength, resilience, and clarity.

Mindfulness sounds easy, and the concept seems simple, but the practice is not, at least not for me. This chapter uncovers the practical steps to integrate mindfulness into your daily life and professional practice, allowing you to thrive in and out of the courtroom. Learn how mindfulness makes a difference in your life, the gifts from practicing law mindfully, and ways to become more mindful in your law practice.

What Is Mindfulness?

Mindfulness is the practice of purposely focusing on the present moment and accepting it without judgment. It means being fully present and aware of where you are and what you're doing without reacting to circumstances or being overwhelmed by what is happening. You know your thoughts and feelings, but don't react or prejudge them. You're free from your past behavior of having a quick emotional response to the circumstances around you. It's a moment-to-moment self-awareness.

This mental discipline allows you to approach your legal work with a clear and non-reactive mindset. Being fully present and attentive in each moment will enable you to make well-informed decisions and enhance your ability to empathize with clients and opposing parties. It reduces the detrimental effects of stress that often accompany the demanding nature of your work. Mindfulness fosters emotional intelligence, which aids you in recognizing and managing emotions as well as understanding the feelings of others.

Here are examples of some things that may happen in your practice where you may tend to react in an unhelpful way:

- The phone rings, and It's that lawyer you cannot stand—the one who always accuses, blames, and attacks for no reason. Will you pick up the phone and argue with him, or ignore his call?

- You may have a paralegal who dropped the ball. She didn't do the assignment she was supposed to do and then called in sick. Now It's on your plate.

- What about when you've had an ongoing disagreement with that attorney? You continue the argument in your head all on your own.

- You focus on what you'll be doing later in the day instead of the present, even when you have an important assignment to work on.

In each situation, a lack of mindfulness increases stress and distraction. This causes less productivity and more anxiety. Who needs that?

Why Be More Mindful?

Stress often causes significant problems for attorneys, including physical and mental health issues. It can lead to headaches, fatigue, sleep problems, depression, eating, immune, and digestive problems. Many lawyers report concerns with anxiety and depression in their careers. A considerable percentage report that they have issues with substance abuse. The legal profession has one of the highest incidences of suicide.

Stress hampers work performance. An overstressed lawyer may make costly mistakes, miss deadlines, overreact to circumstances, be distracted, and have poor focus.

Mindfulness can help with a lot of these problems. Here are some of the primary benefits of mindfulness:

Reduced Stress
Daily events that used to throw you off your game do not bother you as much now.

Improved Focus
You are no longer distracted and complete your work faster and better.

Improved Performance
You're more confident, relaxed, and resilient.

More Self-Awareness
You know what is going on and how it makes you feel.

Better Decision Making

You don't make hasty, rash decisions based on temporary feelings but are more reflective.

Managed Emotions

You stop overreacting, lashing out, and being too reactive.

More Emotional Resilience

You remain calm, clear-headed, and relaxed even when circumstances are challenging.

Improved Relationships

You have more effective communication with your colleagues, family, and friends. Interpersonal connections become more genuine.

Better All-Around

Your well-being improves emotionally and physically.

What About Attorneys?

For lawyers, mindfulness has specific benefits, including:

Enhanced Focus and Concentration

Mindfulness practices cultivate the ability to stay present and focused on the task. This heightened concentration enables you to analyze complex legal issues and strategize effectively.

Reduced Stress and Burnout

The legal profession is highly stressful, with demanding deadlines and high stakes. Mindfulness techniques help you manage stress, prevent burnout, and maintain balance in your professional lives.

Improved Decision-Making

Mindfulness fosters a non-reactive approach to situations, allowing lawyers to make more thoughtful and rational decisions. By staying composed in the face of challenges, you can evaluate options more easily and choose the most appropriate action.

Heightened Emotional Intelligence

Mindfulness practices help you become more attuned to your emotions and those of others. This increased emotional intelligence fosters better communication, empathy, and understanding in interactions with clients, colleagues, and opposing parties.

Effective Communication

Mindfulness encourages active listening and open communication. You become more attentive during client meetings, hearings, and negotiations, leading to stronger connections with clients and better legal representation.

Resilience in Adversity

Setbacks and adversity are common in law practice. Mindfulness fosters mental strength, allowing you to bounce back from setbacks and challenges more effectively.

Increased Creativity

Mindfulness can enhance your creative problem-solving skills by promoting a less rigid and more open mind. You develop innovative legal strategies and approaches to complex legal issues.

Work-Life Balance

Mindfulness helps you draw more explicit boundaries between work and personal life. Being fully present in each domain, you achieve a healthier work-life balance and prevent professional pressures from overwhelming your personal life.

Professional Satisfaction

Mindfulness encourages you to find meaning and purpose in your work beyond financial success. By aligning your legal practice with your values, you experience greater professional fulfillment.

Mindfulness offers a valuable set of tools to navigate the challenges of law practice with greater clarity, resilience, and well-being. By incorporating mindfulness into your daily life, you can excel in your career and lead a more fulfilling and balanced life.

How Can You Learn To Be More Mindful?

Mindfulness fosters an alert, focused, and relaxed state. Deliberately pay attention to the thoughts and sensations you feel. That helps you refocus on the present moment. Observe what you see, hear, think, and feel. Be aware of the emotions you're feeling but without any judgment. Let go of thoughts such as right and wrong, fair and unfair.

It's not easy, but here are some tips to improve your mindfulness:

Stop Your Flight or Flight Habit

Perhaps you are running from circumstances you don't like or preparing for a battle. It's time to stop avoiding and resisting. Those practices only accentuate unpleasant feelings.

Daily Meditation

Regular meditation sessions can significantly improve mindfulness, even just a few minutes daily. Techniques like focused breathing can help quiet your mind, increase self-awareness, and reduce distractions. Find time each day in a quiet place, and focus on breathing. If your attention wanders, refocus back on your breathing. Let the thoughts enter your mind pass without judgment. Try this every day, and gradually increase the length of time you do it.

Mindful Listening

Listening attentively during client meetings, negotiations, or court proceedings can improve understanding and communication. Refrain from interrupting and truly engage with what others are saying.

Mindful Time Management

Apply mindfulness to your daily schedule by prioritizing tasks, setting realistic goals, and focusing on one task at a time. This approach helps prevent overwhelm and improves productivity.

Practice Acceptance

We create much of the stress we feel. We resist people and circumstances. Instead, accept them as being exactly what they're supposed to be. Don't judge them or think about what is right or just or fair; just take reality as being what it is. Then, pause and reflect on your response.

Take Mindfulness Resets

During the day, take several breaks and reset your mind. Whenever you feel overwhelmed or stressed, taking a mindful pause can be helpful. Stop briefly, take a few deep breaths, and re-center before proceeding with the next task.

Journal

Writing down thoughts, emotions, and reflections in a journal can enhance self-awareness and provide a space to process your experiences with greater mindfulness.

Engage in a Daily Gratitude Practice

Each day during your evening resting, think of at least three things that happened during the day for which you're grateful. Let go of the circumstances that caused you stress or were unpleasant.

Conclusion

It's natural to encounter stress in your practice. You can overreact and get distracted and anxious. Relentless challenges and high-pressure situations are the norm. Embracing mindfulness is an indispensable asset for lawyers seeking to thrive personally and professionally. The benefits are profound—enhanced focus, reduced stress, improved decision-making, and heightened emotional intelligence—all leading to a more fulfilled and balanced legal practice. Practicing mindfulness helps you be more aware of the circumstances around you without judgment.

You will become calmer, more focused, productive, and resilient when you become more mindful. By integrating mindfulness into your daily life, you hold the key to unlocking the full potential of the mindful lawyer within you. Mindfulness is not a destination but a continuous process of self-discovery and growth, so be patient when building these new habits and ways of thinking. Work a little daily to embrace the present and the power of mindfulness and witness its profound impact on your life.

Key 6: Compassion

(Empathy in Action: How Compassion Elevates Your Legal Practice)

"Love and compassion are necessities, not luxuries. Without them, humanity cannot survive."
–Dalai Lama

Lawyers often have a reputation for being intelligent, confident, in control, and intensely logical. But sometimes, there's also an unfavorable reputation for being arrogant, insensitive, or poor listeners. That's because we rarely focus on compassion. Why is it critical to be a compassionate lawyer? While conveying a professional image is vital, you should still be authentically human in your practice. Compassion isn't merely an optional addition to your toolkit but an integral force that elevates you personally and enriches the fabric of the legal profession.

Compassion isn't often associated with the intense world of law, but it quietly shapes the true essence of lawyering. Compassion is the beating heart of legal practice, reminding you that behind every case file is a human story brimming with emotions, hopes, and vulnerabilities.

In this chapter, you'll learn what compassion is, how it differs from sympathy and empathy, how to be a more compassionate lawyer, and why striving to be a more compassionate counselor is in your best interest.

What Is Compassion?

Compassion is the feeling you experience when confronted with another's pain and feel motivated to relieve that suffering. Compassion includes the qualities of wisdom, patience, warmth, and kindness.

Compassion is unique, although related to sympathy and empathy. Sympathy means you understand what the other person is feeling. Empathy describes your ability to understand and feel another person's emotions.

Compassion takes empathy and sympathy to the next level. It includes the extra desire to help relieve a situation. When you're compassionate, you empathize with someone struggling and feel compelled to help that person overcome what they're facing. You experience the other person's pain and want to find a way to relieve it.

What Does It Mean To Be Compassionate As A Lawyer?

Being compassionate as a lawyer entails prioritizing empathy, understanding, and support. It acknowledges the human element that permeates every legal case. Compassion benefits your practice in these ways:

Empathetic Listening

Compassionate lawyers actively listen to their clients, allowing them to express their concerns, fears, and hopes. You can better understand your clients' needs and emotions by creating a safe space for open dialogue.

Deep Understanding of Client Stories

Compassion involves recognizing each client has a unique narrative and background. Take the time to learn about your client's experiences and motivations, understanding how these factors impact their legal situation.

Sensitivity to Emotions

Lawyers with compassion understand the emotional nuances of their clients. Acknowledge and validate these emotions, showing sensitivity to your client's stress and challenges.

Transparency and Clear Communication

Compassionate lawyers communicate clearly and understandably. Provide honest assessments of potential outcomes, ensuring clients make informed decisions.

Respect

Compassionate lawyers treat clients, colleagues, and all parties respectfully and with dignity. Foster a collaborative environment, even when representing opposing sides, and always maintain professionalism.

Holistic Approach

Compassion in legal practice involves looking beyond the immediate issue and considering its broader impact on a client's life. Take a holistic view of the situation.

Support During Difficult Times

Lawyers who embody compassion offer emotional support to clients during challenging legal processes. Reassure clients, provide guidance, and serve as a source of strength.

In essence, being compassionate as a lawyer is about merging the principles of justice with the humanity of those seeking your assistance. It requires an unwavering commitment to treating clients as individuals deserving of empathy, respect, and support throughout their legal journey.

Why Should You Be More Compassionate?

There are many benefits to practicing law more compassionately. Here are just some of them:

Client Benefits

Not only do you solve client problems, but when you actively listen to them and are fueled by a desire to relieve a challenging situation, clients genuinely appreciate how caring and helpful you are.

Improved Client Relationships

You'll experience better relationships with your clients. Compassion builds trust and rapport between lawyers and clients. When clients feel understood and supported, they are more open and cooperative, strengthening attorney-client relationships.

Better Communication

Compassionate lawyers excel in clear and empathetic communication. You explain complex legal concepts in understandable terms, ensuring clients are well-informed and making educated decisions about their cases.

Higher Client Satisfaction

When clients feel that you genuinely care about their welfare, they're likelier to be happy with your service and the outcome, regardless of the result.

More Referrals

Your reputation with clients and the community improves drastically when you practice compassionate lawyering. Satisfied clients are more inclined to recommend compassionate lawyers to others in need. You will likely enjoy a positive reputation within the legal community and a steady stream of referrals.

Better Case Resolution

Compassionate lawyers often excel at negotiation and mediation. They can identify common ground and work towards mutually beneficial solutions, leading to faster and less adversarial conflict resolution.

Increased Problem Solving

Compassionate lawyers take the time to thoroughly understand their clients' situations, allowing you to identify underlying issues and provide well-rounded solutions that address not only the legal aspects but also the emotional and practical challenges. Fueled by a desire to help your clients, you become better problem solvers for them and less distracted by the attitude of the other lawyer and other pressures.

Higher Resilience

When you have a passion for helping your clients, you develop greater resilience both personally and as a lawyer. You won't give up. Your desire to help your clients is that powerful.

Reduced Self-Centeredness

When I am at my worst, my focus is on me and what I want. But when I focus on being more compassionate, my attitude toward life is much more selfless and positive. It's no longer about me; it's about the less fortunate person who I can help.

Improved Well-being

Compassion can improve your mental and physical health. Being empathetic and understanding can reduce stress for us. In short, you feel "good" when you empathetically help others solve their problems.

More Fulfillment

Compassionate lawyers often find work more meaningful and fulfilling. Making a positive impact on clients' lives can bring a sense of purpose and satisfaction to your practice. True professional happiness comes when you compassionately solve your clients' problems. You feel more fulfilled when helping others. That fulfillment helps relieve anxiety, which is often a necessary part of legal practice.

Enjoy the Circle of Compassion

When you're compassionate, you feel rewarded. You're more

emotionally satisfied. It causes us to practice more compassion, and we feel more comfortable. It feeds on itself, grows, and grows. Compassionate lawyering creates a beautiful cycle of generosity and empathy.

How Do You Grow Into Being A More Compassionate Attorney?

Lawyers who consistently practice compassion develop strong networks of loyal clients and colleagues. Clients are more satisfied, referring others. You experience more fulfillment and an improved reputation. As a result, more clients are attracted to you and appreciate the value you provide. Your practice grows and becomes more successful.

Here are steps you can follow to build a practice of compassion:

Practice Self-Compassion First

You can sometimes be your own harshest critic. Do you give yourself a tough time when you make a mistake or don't meet your expectations? Compassion begins within yourself. Before you can be compassionate with others, you must be compassionate with yourself.

Avoid Envy

If you envy others and want what they have, you can no longer be compassionate to those in need. Instead, you focus on yourself, desiring what someone else has. Envy prevents you from being human.

Stop Judging

Do you find yourself judging others who are less fortunate? Do you ask— "Why are they struggling? Why do they have so many problems? What is wrong with them?" Discard those feelings. It's not for you to judge the why. Instead, focus on *how* you can be of service.

Actively Listen

Pay close attention to clients and colleagues, Listen without interrupting, show genuine interest, and ask clarifying questions to understand their perspectives fully. Look at the other person in their eyes. Be focused. Empathize with their emotions. Be present with them. Being a good listener is in itself a step towards compassion.

Practice Mindfulness

Practice mindfulness techniques to stay present and attuned to the emotions of others. Regular self-reflection helps you assess your interactions and identify areas for improvement. Be aware of what you're feeling. Notice your thoughts when sliding towards less helpful attitudes. Reset your mind and focus your thoughts on how you can benefit others.

Employ Empathy

Engage in empathy-building exercises like imagining yourself in your client's or colleague's shoes. You better grasp their emotions and challenges.

Focus on the Client

Shift your focus from the legal problem to the individual experiencing it. Understand their goals, fears, and aspirations to tailor your approach accordingly.

Be Intentional

Create a purpose for today to be compassionate with others, to understand and empathize with their feelings, and to be helpful to them. If you begin your day this way, your actions can further your purpose.

Practice Gratitude

Cultivate gratitude for the opportunity to impact people's lives positively. When you're grateful, you're more aware of how blessed you are and how you can serve others. This mindset can reinforce your commitment to compassion.

Journal

Keep a journal to reflect on your interactions, noting moments when you could have been more compassionate, and consider how to improve in similar situations.

Take Small Steps Daily

Look for opportunities to help strangers in need. Do something nice for someone else without getting found out, whether it's opening the door for someone, offering a seat to an older person, consoling a child who fell, buying lunch for the person behind you in line, or helping the other driver who is disabled on the side of the road, These little steps will help you to build the practice of compassion.

Obtain Mentoring

Connect with a mentor who embodies compassionate practices. Their insights and experiences can guide you in incorporating compassion into your work. A wise, empathetic mentor can support you in staying on track with compassion.

Conclusion

Compassion is often not associated with lawyers. Yet, it's one of the most essential traits of a successful, caring attorney. Building empathy is an ongoing journey. Start with small steps and gradually integrate these tools into your daily interactions. Over time, you'll find that incorporating compassion into your legal practice benefits your clients and enhances your professional fulfillment and growth.

Lawyers hold the capacity to uplift and inspire change. Let compassion guide you as you navigate the tapestry of your client's human stories, transforming your practice from a mere transaction of services to a profound understanding and connection. Forge a path where the heart of the law beats in rhythm with the heartbeats of those you serve, painting a canvas of deeply and passionately caring justice.

Key 7: Authenticity

(THE AUTHENTIC LAWYER: ETHICS, INTEGRITY, AND PROFESSIONALISM)

"What we know matters, but who we are matters more."
– Brene Brown

Do you ever feel like you're wearing a mask?

How does that affect you, and how can you change it?

Can there be genuinely authentic attorneys?

While you passionately debate the merits of your cases and where legal decisions shape lives, one enduring principle stands tall as an unwavering beacon of ethical practice: authenticity. The authentic lawyer, guided by integrity and a commitment to truth, holds a formidable key to unlocking the potential for genuine connections and the pursuit of justice.

Lawyers spend so much time creating arguments, posturing, being in charge, and controlling. Maybe you've even been brainwashed to work too hard, never complain, and not set personal boundaries. To be accepted, you may have to act a certain way around the partner or say certain things to others in the firm.

In this chapter, we dive into the heart of legal authenticity, exploring the how and the profound why behind its significance. As you peel back the layers of this fundamental concept, you'll uncover how authenticity nurtures trust, enriches advocacy, and ultimately reshapes the legal landscape with integrity as its guiding compass. It starts by discovering what authenticity means.

What Is Authenticity?

Most dictionaries define authenticity as "the quality of being genuine or real." Many people may have different explanations of authenticity, but most agree that it includes being true to your personality, values, and spirit, regardless of any pressure to act otherwise. It involves being honest with yourself and others and taking responsibility for your mistakes.

You are authentic when you live your life according to your values and goals rather than those of others. Your actions are consistent with your values and your ideals. When you're authentic, you speak honestly and in a healthy way. You can set clear boundaries, avoid toxic environments, and be vulnerable and open without fear.

What About Authenticity for Lawyers

Authenticity encompasses a range of ethical and professional values. Here are some key aspects of authenticity for lawyers:

Honesty and Integrity

Lawyers abide by a code of ethics that requires honesty and truth during interactions with clients, opposing parties, and the courts. We are to provide accurate information, avoid misrepresentations, and disclose conflicts of interest.

Client Communication

Authenticity in client communication means being transparent and clear when discussing legal matters with clients. Lawyers must provide realistic assessments of their clients' cases, including potential risks and outcomes, rather than making unrealistic promises.

Advocacy with Integrity

While lawyers are zealous advocates for their clients, authenticity requires presenting arguments and evidence in good faith and avoiding misleading or deceptive tactics.

Respectful Conduct

Authenticity extends to treating all parties respectfully and courteously, regardless of their position or background. We should respect the dignity and rights of clients, opposing counsel, judges, and court staff.

Confidentiality

Lawyers must maintain the confidentiality of client information and only disclose it as necessary for the representation or as required by law. Being authentic means respecting the trust clients place in us and protecting their privacy.

Ethical Decision-Making

Authentic lawyers approach ethical dilemmas thoughtfully, prioritizing the interests of justice and a client's best interests over personal gain or convenience.

By embodying authenticity in law practice, lawyers adhere to professional responsibilities and build trust with clients, colleagues, and the public, ultimately contributing to a more just and equitable legal system.

The Problem With Authenticity In the Legal Profession

Historically, the legal profession has struggled with authenticity, including the reputation for being disingenuous, misleading, and perhaps fake. It may have come from the essence of the law practice, taking one side of an issue and creating arguments to support it.

Part of the problem stems from the competitiveness of legal

practice. We get a job in the firm and do not want to complain or set boundaries. We say yes to too much, often more than we can. We "toe the company line" and do not want to make waves. We want to be one of those who succeed in making partners in a competitive environment. Even when you're overwhelmed or asked to do something uncomfortable with your values, you do it because you feel you must do it. The model where young lawyers work themselves much too hard to move up the ladder to become partners isn't practical for either the lawyer or the law firm.

Then, you want to develop your book of business. You want to bring in more clients to show your value to your firm or to create more revenues. As a result, you sometimes present a different image to different clients to bring in new clients. You're open sometimes about what clients you represent. We may represent clients incompatible with your values, or you may take stances inconsistent with how you want to practice law.

And if you're in litigation, It's always a game of posturing and frequently hiding the truth. We always try to create a specific image that may differ from the facts. That is the nature of being a successful litigator.

What is the upshot of this? We begin to feel frustrated, unfulfilled, and stressed. You're unhappy with what you're doing because you act in ways that are different from who you are.

While authenticity is a commendable trait, challenges are associated with its practice in our profession. These issues arise due to the delicate balance between authenticity and the strict ethical and professional obligations that you must uphold. Here are a few areas where authenticity can create problems in the legal profession:

Attorney-Client Privilege: While authenticity encourages open communication, lawyers must also maintain strict confidentiality under the attorney-client privilege. Balancing the need for transparency with preserving client confidentiality can be challenging.

Zealous Advocacy vs. Authenticity: Lawyers must provide

zealous advocacy for their clients, which may sometimes conflict with personal values or principles. Striking a balance between zealous advocacy and staying true to one's authentic self can be delicate.

Ethical Considerations in Negotiations: In negotiations, lawyers may use persuasive techniques to achieve favorable outcomes. Balancing authenticity with ethical negotiation practices is essential to avoid crossing ethical boundaries.

Despite these potential challenges, authenticity remains valuable for lawyers when practiced with adherence to professional ethics and responsibilities. Striving for authenticity can lead to stronger client relationships, increased trust, and more meaningful and fulfilling legal practice.

Why Is It Important To Be Authentic As An Attorney?

The old model of "Grin and bear it" doesn't work. Stifling your true self to succeed in the firm and bring in clients, no matter the conflict between representing them and your values, leads to frustration, unhappiness, and stress. The legal field is growing and changing. You're discovering that wellness and integrity for lawyers are critical.

These are some crucial benefits of being authentic in the legal profession:

Client Satisfaction

Authenticity fosters trust between lawyers and clients. Clients who perceive their attorneys as genuine, honest, and transparent are likelier to confide in them, share crucial information, and confidently follow their legal advice. Clients are entitled to know who you are and how you intend to represent them. You form a more genuine professional connection when you demonstrate your true selves to your clients. Legal representation is an intensely personal and intimate relationship. Our clients are happier when they know who they are getting, what you are like, and how you will represent them.

Better Performance

You're a better attorney when you are true to yourself acting consistently with your values. An authentic lawyer is better equipped to present a compelling case in court. By being true to your convictions, you passionately advocate for your clients while maintaining credibility with judges, juries, and opposing counsel. Also, when you enter your firm's doors without worrying about acting in a certain way but can speak your truth, suggest your ideas, and be open about your concerns or frustrations, you are happier and more successful.

A Good Reputation

Sadly, our standing with many is not what we want. We are perceived as too expensive, creating fights and making arguments. Authenticity contributes to a lawyer's positive reputation within the legal community and among clients. Word-of-mouth referrals and recommendations are more likely when clients and colleagues view you as trustworthy and genuine. When straightforward with your client and the opposing party, you can improve the legal profession's reputation, one attorney at a time.

Personal Fulfillment

When you do the work you love with people who value you, act consistently with your values, and represent clients you appreciate and who appreciate you, you achieve personal fulfillment that many of us have yet to experience. However, when your work as an attorney conflicts with your true nature or requires you to act in ways inconsistent with your values, you feel frustrated and unhappy on a profoundly personal level. Authenticity helps you to achieve the fulfillment that you all deserve.

Greater Success

Being liked by everyone is not the key to success. Our client understands you, who you are, and how you will manage their matter. That transparency creates a stronger attorney-client relationship and attracts other clients to us. I won't be everyone's cup of tea. My style may not be what they want. But, by being authentic, I will find the right client who works well with me and appreciates how I handle their matters and solve their problems. The key to building your law practice is attracting clients who are a good fit for us.

For example, In my family law practice, I tell all my prospective clients two things at the beginning of our call. First, I am not a pitbull who wants to fight, create arguments, and harm the other spouse. Instead, as a firm and strong advocate, I aim to be courteous and respectful and to solve the issues as quickly and promptly as possible. I also do not always judge my clients, but I tell them I want to represent someone respectful and responsible. I avoid the problem of clients who expect me to be something I am not.

Health and Wellness

A life of authentic and genuine relationships is a satisfying one. Lawyers can maintain a healthier work-life balance when they are true to themselves. When you pretend to be something you are not, when you are not speaking your truth, and when you feel taken advantage of, you suffer stress, frustration, and burnout. Wellness matters in the legal profession. Practicing authentically as an attorney creates an environment where you are fulfilled, successful, and physically and emotionally healthy.

How Do You Achieve Greater Authenticity As An Attorney?

Here are steps you can apply, starting today, building greater authenticity and create personal freedom for yourself:

Take a Personal Inventory

Step back. Reflect. Take time to identify and clarify your core values as a lawyer. Consider the principles most important to you in your legal practice, such as honesty, integrity, empathy, and justice. Understanding your values will serve as a foundation for your authentic approach. What is important to you? What are your core values that matter? What type of people or endeavors make you feel most energized? What persons or situations make you feel angry or frustrated? Try to determine what values and characteristics are significant to you.

Align Actions with Values

Once you have identified your most important values, ascertain what is inconsistent with those values in your life. Is there a discrepancy between who you are now and what you want to be? Do you pretend to be something you're not at work? Do you put on a mask to avoid being seen as you are? Is there a discrepancy between who you are and how people see you? Actual authenticity results when the person you are is the same as the person you portray yourself as and the person others see.

Embrace Self-awareness.

Engage in regular self-reflection to gain insights into your thoughts, emotions, and behaviors. Recognize your strengths and areas for improvement, and be open to acknowledging any areas where you may have fallen short of being authentic. Regardless of what is happening around you, being mindful of how you feel is a key to authenticity. As you develop your mindfulness, you'll begin to understand when you were being inauthentic.

Be Honest and Speak Your Truth.

Create open and honest communication with those around you. Be attentive when others speak to you by listening carefully and maintaining good eye contact. But be willing to say "no" when you need to. Express your needs and your desires honestly and with confidence. Honest and open communication is both freeing and healthy. The key is to say what you mean and mean what you say while understanding and respecting the other person's needs and feelings.

Act Consistently With Your Values.

Avoid compromising your authenticity to conform to societal or professional expectations. Your fulfillment, your health, and your satisfaction are too important. Whatever your core values are, make sure that others are aware of them and that they do not force you to act inconsistently with them. Always try to be true to yourself. Authenticity requires that you live according to your core values and beliefs.

Establish Your Boundaries.

Many of us need to set healthy boundaries between work and home life. Without limits, you receive client calls on Friday night and Sunday morning and are deluged with last-minute demands by partners to work late. You need boundaries so you can establish a balance in your lives between your work and your leisure. To be authentic, those around you need to know what you can and cannot do and what is too much. It's okay to say no.

Develop a Healthy Support Network.

Create healthy professional and nonprofessional relationships with those you respect and with similar values. Those relationships support you when you need it the most. Develop a relationship with a mentor who can be a sounding board, help you reset, and assist you in understanding what is causing your frustration. Surround yourself with supportive people who lift and encourage you to be your best. You're often defined by those you surround yourself with. Your most meaningful relationships should include those with similar values, ideals, and passions. A strong support network helps you clarify who you are and where you want to be.

Conclusion

Developing a culture of authenticity is essential. Embracing authenticity is not merely a choice but a moral imperative—a call to stand steadfast in the face of challenges, wield your legal acumen guided by unwavering integrity, and champion the values that fortify the bedrock of a just society. You are an expert problem solver who has your client's best interests at heart.

Acting authentically allows you to be more successful and fulfilled. Nothing is more critical to developing your freedom than being open, genuine, and authentic. Let us unite under authenticity, empowering each other to uphold the sacred trust bestowed upon us, enriching our communities, and shaping a legacy of truth, compassion, and lasting impact for generations.

Key 8: Emotional Intelligence

(The Power of Emotional Intelligence: A Lawyer's Secret Weapon)

"Between stimulus and response, there's a space. In that space lies our freedom and power to choose our response. In our response lies our growth and freedom."
– Viktor E. Frankl

Have you ever had a crisis at work, someone made a mistake, and the boss gets very angry, perhaps screaming, reacts rashly, and blames the person at fault?

Never seeing his part in it?

Or, in the same scenario, have you ever seen the leader respond thoughtfully, be empathetic with the person who made the mistake, and incorporate the team in finding a solution to achieve better results in the future?

What is the difference between these two scenarios? It's what is frequently called "emotional intelligence," often referred to as EI. As lawyers, we are well-versed in the intricacies of the law and equipped with sharp analytical minds to navigate complex cases and debates. However, you must not forget the immense impact of emotional intelligence on your effectiveness as an advocate and counselor. In your fast-paced and demanding profession, understanding and harnessing the power of EI can be the key to achieving success in your practice and forging lasting connections with clients, colleagues, and the community.

In this chapter, we explore the multifaceted world of emotional intelligence for lawyers, discussing why It's an indispensable skill for excelling in law practice. I will explain what emotional intelligence is, its characteristics, how someone behaves when acting with low emotional intelligence, how it benefits us, and how to develop your emotional intelligence skills.

What Is Emotional Intelligence?

Emotional intelligence (also referred to as "EI") refers to the ability to understand and manage your own emotions and those of others you interact with. People with high emotional intelligence know their feelings and emotions and how they can affect others around them.

When you have good emotional intelligence, you understand, use, and manage your emotions positively to relieve stress, communicate more effectively, empathize with others, withstand challenges, and resolve conflict. Emotional intelligence helps you build stronger relationships, succeed more in your profession, and achieve your career goals. It promotes your being more aware of your feelings. You act on your vision and make responsible choices about what matters most.

Lawyers with high emotional intelligence can navigate challenging situations with composure, build strong relationships with clients, colleagues, and opposing counsel, and make sound decisions with a balanced blend of logic and empathy. For lawyers, emotional intelligence involves self-awareness, which means being conscious of one's emotions, strengths, weaknesses, and triggers. This self-awareness enables lawyers to manage their emotions effectively and prevent them from clouding their judgment or interfering with their professional duties.

Additionally, emotional intelligence entails being attuned to the emotions of others, such as clients, witnesses, and colleagues. By displaying empathy and understanding, lawyers can establish rapport, create a safe environment for open communication, and better comprehend the needs and concerns of their clients. Moreover, emotional intelligence for lawyers involves the skill of emotional regulation, which is the ability to manage and channel emotions appropriately. This includes staying composed under pressure, dealing with conflict constructively, and maintaining a level-headed approach when faced with adversarial situations.

The Five Primary Attributes Of Emotional Intelligence

These are generally considered the most essential attributes of emotional intelligence:

1. **Self-management.** You control your emotions, impulses, and reactions. You respond appropriately to the feelings of others. You restrain the urge to act impulsively. You're flexible and adapt to different circumstances. You seldom verbally attack others, do not make rash or emotional decisions, or jump to conclusions. You keep your emotions under control.

2. **Self-awareness.** You recognize your own emotions, values, and motivations. You understand how they affect your feelings and actions. You know your strengths and weaknesses and have self-confidence. You're aware of how you feel. You know how your emotions and your actions affect those around you. You respond humbly to situations.

3. **Motivation.** A person with high emotional intelligence is highly motivated and passionate about personal development. You strive to accomplish your personal goals of success. You want to satisfy your vision, not because of money or recognition but because it helps you grow Individually.

4. **Empathy**. You consider and empathize with the feelings and emotions of those around you. You think about how you would feel and respond if you were in their situation. You're not self-centered. You understand the emotions of the other person. You are compassionate about the circumstances they are experiencing. You do not judge other people. You know that you are all doing your best in your circumstances.

5. **Social skills**. You know how to maintain good relationships with other people, you communicate clearly, you work well as part of a team, you inspire other people, and you know how to manage conflict. You're adept at active listening and learning how to develop a connection with those around you. You maintain good eye contact, listen carefully, and have welcoming body language. You understand the needs of others when there's a situation of conflict. You're good at managing change and resolving conflicts. You lead others by example. You know how to get others to support you and embrace change and growth.

If you're emotionally intelligent, you:

- Accept constructive criticism. And you're responsible for managing your tasks.

- Don't judge others.

- Understand why you take certain actions and feel specific ways.

- Are a great listener.

- Openly share your feelings.

- Know how to say no at the right time.

- Understand, learn from, and move forward when you make a mistake.

- Find solutions to problems that satisfy the needs of the various parties.

- Are adept at resolving conflict and are empathetic with others.

What Does Low Emotional Intelligence Look Like?

That all sounds wonderful. But what are the characteristics of a person with low emotional intelligence? And have you ever encountered this in your law practice?

Highly opinionated

A person with lower emotional intelligence thinks he is always right. He frequently argues with other people. He is not interested in listening to the opinions of others. He is not good at expressing emotions and responding to the opinions or feelings of other people. He has difficulty learning and growing from his own mistakes.

Insensitive

This person always says the wrong thing at the wrong time. He makes a joke when It's entirely inappropriate. He is unaware of the feelings of other people. He lacks empathy for others.

Blames Others

He is not accountable for his actions. He is always looking for someone to blame. Nothing is ever his fault. He always wants to be correct. He is the first person to point the finger at someone else.

Unmotivated

A person with low emotional intelligence is frequently unmotivated. He has a hard time handling challenges and coping with emotional situations. He often hides his feelings.

Emotionally Explosive

He cannot control or manage his own emotions. He "flies off the handle." When he is upset, he explodes emotionally and negatively.

He often has uncontrollable emotional outbursts. He is easily triggered and upset. He explodes in a passionate tirade when things do not go his way. He doesn't understand what he is feeling or why.

Self-Centered

He always wants to be the center of attention. He thinks he is better than everyone else. He always wants to tell you how good he is. His achievements are always better than yours. He wants to do most of the talking and almost always about himself. He is not interested in asking about you or how you're feeling.

Relationship Problems

He tends to have few friends because he cannot develop an emotional connection with other people. His relationships are frequently unsuccessful and short-lived.

Why Should You Develop Your Emotional Intelligence?

Emotional intelligence offers many benefits for lawyers, positively impacting their professional and personal lives. Some of the key benefits include:

Improved Client Relationships

Lawyers with high emotional intelligence can connect with their clients more deeply by understanding their emotions and concerns. Building strong client relationships based on trust and empathy fosters better communication and helps lawyers tailor their approach to better meet their clients' needs.

Effective Communication

Emotional intelligence enhances lawyers' communication skills, allowing them to articulate complex legal concepts in a more relatable manner. This skill is precious when explaining legal matters to clients, juries, or other parties involved in a case.

Conflict Resolution

Lawyers with emotional intelligence can navigate conflicts and negotiations more effectively. By understanding their own emotions and those of others, they can approach disputes calmly, actively listen to opposing viewpoints, and find mutually beneficial solutions.

Reduced Stress and Burnout

Emotional intelligence enables lawyers to manage stress more effectively. They can identify early signs of burnout and implement strategies to cope with the demands of their profession, leading to better overall well-being and job satisfaction.

Enhanced Decision-Making

By considering rational and emotional aspects, emotionally intelligent lawyers make more well-rounded and balanced decisions. They are less likely to be swayed by biases or impulsiveness, resulting in more thoughtful and practical client choices.

Leadership and Teamwork

Lawyers with solid emotional intelligence are influential leaders. They can inspire and motivate their teams, foster a positive work environment, and encourage collaboration among colleagues.

Empathetic Legal Representation

Emotional intelligence enables lawyers to approach their work more empathetically. They can understand the emotional impact of legal issues on their client's lives and provide compassionate and supportive legal representation.

Better Advocacy

Emotional intelligence enhances a lawyer's ability to read the emotions and body language of judges, witnesses, and opposing counsel during trials and hearings. This insight helps them adjust their arguments and strategies in real-time, potentially swaying the case outcome.

Client Loyalty and Referrals

Satisfied clients are likelier to recommend a lawyer who displays emotional intelligence and genuinely cares about their well-being. Positive word-of-mouth referrals can significantly benefit a lawyer's practice and reputation.

Adaptability and Resilience

Emotionally intelligent lawyers are better equipped to handle the ups and downs of their profession. They can adapt to changing circumstances, bounce back from setbacks, and maintain a positive attitude throughout their legal careers.

Emotional intelligence equips you with essential skills to excel in your profession and foster meaningful connections with clients and colleagues. By harnessing the power of emotional intelligence, you can elevate your legal practice and achieve tremendous success and fulfillment in your practice.

How Do You Build Greater Emotional Intelligence?

We see the benefits of emotional intelligence. You perform better in your career and are more successful. We feel better, both physically and mentally. We have stronger relationships. We connect with other people and the world around us. So, how do you become more emotionally intelligent?

Reflect Before Responding

When presented with a challenge, constantly choose to take a step back, pause and reflect. Refrain from reacting quickly. Evaluate your emotions and those of the other party. Consider why you feel that way when you feel a strong emotion. Understanding your feelings increases your emotional awareness. Reflect on how your emotions influence your decisions and behaviors. Choose an appropriate response.

Practice Empathy

Put yourself in the other person's shoes. Try to understand what they are feeling and why. Consider how you would feel if you were in their circumstances. Express your understanding of their feelings.

Develop Your Listening Skills

You must first pay close attention to understand the other person's feelings. Listen carefully. Look the other person in the eyes, have an open demeanor, and pay attention to their words and body language.

Be Accountable and Responsible

If you make a mistake, own up to it. Accept responsibility for your actions or choices that did not work out well. Do not blame.

Commit to Your Goals

Understand where you want to get to and why. Know that there will be challenges along the way and that you can learn and grow from each of them.

Praise Often

Compliment others when appropriate. Learn how to praise others when deserved.

Be Mindful

Be aware of the emotions and feelings of others and yourself. Be present and open to both understanding your feelings and those around you. Focus your attention on the present moment without any judgment.

Learn From Your Mistakes

If you handled something wrong or did not respond appropriately, consider what happened and what you learned. Reflect on how you'll handle the situation differently the next time.

Manage Conflict

See conflict as a way to grow closer to the other person involved. Disagreements are inevitable and can lead to growth. See what you can learn in each conflict. Look for a mutual resolution that satisfies both parties. Build trust with the other parties involved by seeking a common solution.

Seek Support from Coaches

Working with a coach who understands emotional intelligence can provide personalized guidance in improving your emotional intelligence skills.

Conclusion

In the dynamic world of law, where intellect and expertise are essential, emotional intelligence emerges as the silent force that sets exceptional lawyers apart. Remember that while you may fight legal battles in courtrooms, you win the most profound victories in your clients' and colleagues' hearts and minds. Cultivating emotional intelligence is not merely a luxury but a necessity in a profession that demands empathy, adaptability, and unwavering integrity. Embrace emotional intelligence as a guide toward a future where law and empathy walk hand in hand, weaving a tapestry of compassion, equity, and true legal excellence.

Key 9: Growth Mindset

(Cultivating a Growth Mindset: Empowering Lawyers for Succes)

*"If you're unwilling to learn, no one can help you.
If you're determined to learn, no one can stop you."*
– Zig Ziglar

**Would you prefer to stick to your habits
and well-known routines?**

Or do you have a passion for learning new things?

**Are you someone who believes you
have certain traits and talents that are
fundamentally unchangeable?**

**Do you have the skills you have and can use but
cannot develop new ones?**

**Or do you believe you can grow, change,
learn, and develop?**

That is the difference between a growth mindset and a fixed mindset. To succeed as you want, you must develop a growth mindset.

In the ever-evolving world of law, where challenges abound, and success hinges on adaptability and continuous learning, having a growth mindset is not just advantageous – it's essential. A growth mindset empowers lawyers to embrace challenges, persist in the face of setbacks, and unlock their true potential. It's the mindset that believes in the capacity for growth, development, and improvement, enabling legal professionals to excel in their careers and make a lasting impact.

Keep reading to explore the significance of a growth mindset for lawyers and explore practical strategies to foster and nurture this mindset. By understanding the power of embracing growth and employing specific techniques, you can embark on a transformative journey to enhance your professional abilities and overall well-being and satisfaction in the legal field.

What Is a Fixed Mindset?

When you have a fixed mindset, you believe your intelligence, talents, and skills are fixed and unchangeable. Individuals with fixed mindsets believe that their qualities and abilities are predetermined. They view them as fixed traits that they cannot improve. If you're not good at something, you believe you will never be good at it. You have set your mind on the fact there are certain things you just are not good at. They are not in your wheelhouse. In a fixed mindset, everything is about success or failure. You may give up because the outcome is not what you wanted.

People with a fixed mindset often avoid challenges because they fear failure or believe their abilities are limited. They may see effort as fruitless because they think their skills are set and will not strengthen through practice or learning. Setbacks and criticism can be particularly challenging for individuals with a fixed mindset, as they interpret them as reflections of their inherent limitations rather than growth opportunities.

A fixed mindset can hinder a lawyer's development and success. It may lead to resistance to new challenges, a fear of making mistakes, and a reluctance to seek feedback or learn from failures. The fixed mindset can limit professional growth and prevent lawyers from reaching their full potential.

These examples highlight the mindset and behaviors of a fixed mindset:

Avoiding Challenges

Individuals with a fixed mindset avoid challenges because they fear failure or believe their abilities are limited. They may prefer to stay within their comfort zones and avoid situations that may challenge their existing skills or knowledge.

Belief in Fixed Abilities

People with a fixed mindset believe their abilities and talents are fixed traits that cannot be significantly developed or improved. They may think they are inherently "good" or "bad" at specific skills or subjects without considering the growth potential.

Giving Up Easily

Those with a fixed mindset may quickly give up or become disheartened when faced with setbacks or obstacles. They may interpret failures as indications of their inherent limitations rather than as opportunities for growth.

Ignoring or Rejecting Feedback

Individuals with a fixed mindset may resist feedback, mainly if it involves constructive criticism or points out areas for improvement. They may view feedback as a personal attack rather than an opportunity to learn and develop.

Seeking Validation

People with a fixed mindset may prioritize seeking validation or proving themselves over the process of learning and growth. They may be more concerned with being perceived as intelligent, talented, or successful rather than focusing on continuous improvement.

Feeling Threatened by Others' Success:
Individuals with a fixed mindset may feel threatened or envious of others' achievements. Instead of being inspired or learning from flourishing individuals, they may view their success as a reflection of their inadequacy.

Resisting Change
People with a fixed mindset may resist change and cling to familiar routines and ways of doing things. They may be hesitant to explore new methods or ideas, fearing they may challenge their existing abilities or knowledge.

It's easy to see how a fixed mindset hinders your progress and success.

What is a Growth Mindset?

A growth mindset believes that one's abilities, intelligence, and talents can be developed and improved through dedication, hard work, perseverance, and learning from failure. It's the mindset that embraces challenges, sees setbacks as opportunities for growth, and believes in the potential for continuous improvement.

Individuals with a growth mindset understand their abilities are not fixed traits but skills and qualities that grow over time. They view effort as a crucial component in achieving success and approach obstacles with resilience and a willingness to learn. Instead of being discouraged by setbacks or criticism, those with a growth mindset see them as opportunities to learn, adapt, and improve.

If you have a growth mindset, you value what you do, regardless of the outcome. You handle new problems, develop skills, and learn new talents. Persons with a growth mindset thrive on the challenges they face. You don't see failures as failures; instead, they are opportunities for growth and development. Your skills and talents may improve.

A growth mindset is critical for lawyers as it allows us to continually expand our legal knowledge, refine our skills, and adapt to the ever-changing landscape of law.

With a growth mindset, you:

- Embrace challenges as opportunities to develop new skills, expand your knowledge, and push your boundaries.

- Understand that success requires dedicated effort and perseverance.

- Are willing to put in the effort to achieve your goals.

- Are not discouraged by failure but view it as a valuable learning experience.

- Are open to constructive criticism, use it to identify areas for improvement, and strive to grow and enhance your skills continuously.

- Prioritize learning and personal growth rather than seeking validation or proving yourself.

- Appreciate the success and accomplishments of others. Instead of feeling threatened or envious, you see successful individuals as sources of inspiration and motivation.

Why Is It Important To Have A Growth Mindset?

Having a growth mindset is crucial for lawyers. Our profession is dynamic and constantly evolving. The business is becoming more challenging, technology is growing, and the landscape is continuously changing. A growth mindset allows us to embrace these changes as opportunities for learning and development rather than obstacles.

Secondly, you must remain resilient in the face of challenges and setbacks. A growth mindset equips you with the mental fortitude to persevere when faced with complex cases, demanding clients, unfavorable outcomes, or challenging partners. It enables you to view setbacks as valuable learning experiences and to analyze your mistakes, identify areas for improvement, and bounce back stronger.

Moreover, a growth mindset promotes a continuous learning

and improvement mindset. When you have a growth mindset, you understand that personal and professional development is a lifelong journey. You invest time and effort into expanding your knowledge and refining your skills.

Additionally, a growth mindset fosters innovation and creativity in legal practice. By approaching legal issues with an open and flexible attitude, you can think outside the box, explore alternative strategies, and find innovative solutions for your clients. You're not constrained by conventional thinking or self-imposed limitations, allowing you to tackle legal challenges innovatively and effectively.

Lastly, a growth mindset enhances your overall well-being and job satisfaction. It promotes a positive attitude, resilience, and a sense of personal fulfillment. Lawyers with a growth mindset are more likely to experience pleasure from their work, enjoy the learning process, and maintain a healthy work-life balance.

How Do We Develop a Growth Mindset?

We can all see the benefits of having a growth mindset. Such a mindset is critical to your growth and success. But how can you develop a growth mindset? Here are some helpful tools:

Be Aware of Your Mindset Voice

If you tell yourself when you fail, it's time to give up, then you may be operating out of a fixed mindset. You must develop an awareness of your mindset voice to change it and develop your desired attitude.

Understand That You Have a Choice

Our fixed mindset says to quit or not try so you don't fail. But you have a choice. You can choose what perspectives you have. Understand that that inner voice is something you control.

Choose a Growth Mindset

When those negative thoughts enter your head, instead of thinking, "If this doesn't work at first, I will quit," change your view. Look at a setback as an opportunity to learn.

Do Not Seek Approval From Others

A fixed mindset worries about what others think of us, whether they see us as failures if our matter doesn't work out how we want. Their thoughts do not matter. Instead, you should focus on yourself, your goals, your visions, and your growth.

Look at Challenges As Opportunities

Do not give in to the fear of failure. Every new challenge is an opportunity to learn, grow your skill set, and analyze mistakes. Whenever you have an obstacle, you're closer to achieving success.

You're "Learning", Not "Failing."

Too often, you can view yourself as a failure when something doesn't work out. Instead, look and see what you can learn from what happened. Analyze what went wrong, identify areas for improvement, and use this knowledge to adjust your approach moving forward. You will be much more successful if you tell yourself you've learned something new whenever you face a challenge.

Embrace Challenges

Seek out challenging cases or projects that push your boundaries and expand your skills. Develop a new practice area. Embrace the opportunity to learn and grow through these challenges.

Seek Feedback

Seek feedback from mentors, colleagues, and clients. Embrace constructive criticism as an opportunity for growth and improvement. Incorporate feedback into your practice and make adjustments accordingly.

Emphasize Effort and Process

Focus on your effort and progress rather than on outcomes.

Recognize that growth comes from consistent effort, perseverance, and a willingness to learn from successes and failures.

Develop Resilience
Build resilience by reframing challenges as opportunities, developing coping mechanisms for stress, and cultivating a positive mindset. Practice self-care to maintain a healthy work-life balance and enhance overall well-being.

Develop a Sense of Purpose
Believe that there's something greater than yourself. Understand that you have a role to fulfill, a way to serve your clients, and a mission to support your profession and contribute to society. Believe that there's an essential reason for taking on a challenge.

Act On Your Growth Mindset
Now that you have chosen to accept challenges and understand that failures are simply an opportunity to learn, get into action. Follow through with those actions. As you take on new challenges, your growth mindset will develop. You'll learn from your mistakes, accept them, and approach your vision of success.

Conclusion

As lawyers, a growth mindset is critical. By embracing a growth mindset, you open yourself to infinite possibilities, transcend limitations, and achieve remarkable personal and professional growth. Cultivate an attitude that sees challenges as stepping stones, failures as lessons, and growth as an ongoing journey. This can reshape the legal profession, unleash potential, and impact the lives of those you serve. The power to unlock your potential lies within you; a growth mindset is the key.

Key 10: The Law of Attraction

*"Decide what you want. Believe you can have it. Believe
you deserve it and believe it's possible for you."*
– Jack Canfield

**Are you ever in a mindset where you think
negative thoughts and expect poor results, and
that's what happens?**

**Alternatively, have you ever envisioned
success, an excellent result, or victory, and
that has occurred?**

As a lawyer, you navigate complex cases and strive for favorable outcomes. Yet, one concept holds the potential to reshape your approach to the legal world—the Law of Attraction. In this chapter, we explore how the power of positive thinking, visualization, and purposeful intention can harmonize with your legal pursuits. In this unique fusion of pragmatism and possibility, we explore how attorneys can harness the principles of the Law of Attraction to enhance their practice, cultivate resilience, and forge deeper connections with clients and colleagues. Whatever your experience, prepare to uncover insights that could reshape your mindset and your entire approach to the profession.

What is the Law of Attraction?

The Law of Attraction is a belief that positive or negative thoughts bring about corresponding positive or negative experiences in a person's life. In essence, it proposes that like attracts like, meaning that the energy and ideas you put into the universe will return similar powers and experiences to you. It's based on the philosophy that positive energy attracts success in all areas of your life. The concept is that the energy of your thoughts manifests in your experiences.

Proponents of the Law of Attraction often emphasize the power of visualization, affirmations, and maintaining a positive mindset. They suggest that by focusing on your goals and desires with solid belief and intention, you can manifest those desires into reality. However, it's important to note that the Law of Attraction is controversial, as scientific evidence supporting its claims is limited, and many critics view it as pseudoscience.

While the Law of Attraction can be a motivational tool for some people, it's crucial to maintain a balanced perspective and recognize that achieving goals typically involves a combination of focused effort, planning, and, sometimes, a bit of luck.

Is the Law of Attraction Real?

Proponents of the Law of Attraction argue that positive thinking, visualization, and intention can influence outcomes by shaping one's mindset and actions. On the other hand, critics often point out that the Law of Attraction can oversimplify complex life situations, neglect external factors, and lack empirical validation. I'm not aware of any scientific studies that prove it's effective. Having said that, the concept of the Law of Attraction unquestionably serves us.

Here are two simple examples from my life. I learned to ride a bike at a much older age than typical, 50 years old. I learned to ride at Kiawah Island, S.C., where there are some fantastic bike trails, many of which had pretty narrow bridges over lagoons. When I was learning to ride, if I looked at the rails on the side of the bridge, I would always ride into them. But if, instead, my vision was straight ahead to the open space past the bridge. I quickly rode through the middle of the bridge – what I thought about created the result.

And as you know, I am an avid golfer. What I focus on directly impacts my results when I play a tight or narrow hole. If I see the trees lining the fairway, invariably, that is where I hit the ball into the trees. But if instead I focus on a tiny target in the middle of the fairway. I am much more likely to hit the ball straight.

It doesn't matter if the Law of Attraction is a scientific fact. What I know is that your thoughts directly affect your results.

Pitfalls of the Law of Attraction

Utilizing the Law of Attraction in your life is very beneficial. However, there are some pitfalls of which you should be aware:

First, you should never think that if you simply believe something good will happen, it will. We still have to put forth the effort. Set your goals, be committed, have a plan, overcome challenges, and be persistent.

Secondly, you should never blame yourself when negative things happen. You shouldn't think, "If only I thought something different, this would not have occurred!" We will run into obstacles outside of our control. We may have a setback despite our best actions and thoughts. What you should do, though, is look at the positive in each of those occurrences. I have learned that every hurdle or adverse event has a powerful silver lining. It was precisely what it was supposed to be. When that challenging obstacle presents itself, don't blame yourself for not having the right thoughts; instead, look for the positive in each of those hurdles and see what you can do to overcome them. How you respond to those challenges is precisely what makes us stronger.

Also, while a positive mindset is valuable, legal success requires expertise, thorough research, strong analytical skills, and effective advocacy. The Law of Attraction alone cannot replace these foundational aspects of legal practice. In addition, while positive thinking can be helpful, it's crucial to maintain a realistic under-standing of legal outcomes. Not all cases will have the desired outcome solely based on positive intentions.

Gifts of the Law of Attraction

When you focus your thoughts on your vision rather than your frustrations, you will unquestionably be more successful. What you think about is what you tend to get more of. If you believe you will fail, you will likely. If you think you will succeed, you're more likely to.

Here is another golf analogy: When I'm hitting a shot over the lake onto the green when I focus on the lake and think I won't be able to hit over it, I very frequently end up at the bottom of the lake. On the other hand, when my focus is on the pin, and I see a successful shot landing near it, I am much more likely to hit my shot safely onto the green and likely near the hole.

My thoughts do not guarantee success, particularly with-out serious effort on my part. However, positive thoughts will improve your mental well-being. We will be more confident, open to tremendous success, and willing to take on a new challenge. Optimistic thoughts will improve your health, create happiness, and result in more successful results.

But specifically, how can the Law of Attraction benefit lawyers? Here are some possibilities:

Positive Mindset

Maintaining a positive mindset can help lawyers approach their work more confidently and resiliently. This positive outlook can influence interactions with clients, colleagues, and opponents, lead-ing to more productive and respectful relationships.

Motivation and Goal Setting

The Law of Attraction encourages setting clear and specific goals while visualizing your achievement. Lawyers who set goals for their practice, cases, and professional development may be more motivated to work consistently toward them.

Visualization

Visualizing successful outcomes can help lawyers mentally prepare for cases, negotiations, and other legal challenges. This practice can enhance your confidence and poise when presenting arguments and making critical decisions.

Stress Management

The Law of Attraction emphasizes reducing negative thoughts and stress. Lawyers who adopt mindfulness and positive affirmations may experience reduced stress levels, allowing them to think more clearly and make better decisions.

Client Relations

Applying the principles of the Law of Attraction can improve lawyer-client relationships. Maintaining a positive and empathetic attitude can build trust, making clients feel understood and supported throughout the legal process.

Preparation and Focus

The Law of Attraction underscores the power of focused attention. Lawyers can use this principle to enhance their preparation for cases, ensuring you're fully engaged and attentive to the details that matter.

Resilience and Adaptability

Believing in the possibility of positive outcomes can help lawyers maintain strength in the face of challenges. Instead of dwelling on setbacks, you can focus on solutions and keep moving forward.

How Can the Law of Attraction Work for You?

The Law of Attraction can help us succeed in many areas of our life. Here are nine tangible steps for you to follow to help create that success and personal freedom you crave:

Be Grateful

Regularly express gratitude for the opportunities, successes, and experiences you've had in your legal career. Gratitude can amplify positive energy. An attitude of gratitude is critical to your success. We truly appreciate the many blessings in your life. We think positive thoughts about the present, which helps to create better results for us.

Be Mindful

Practice mindfulness to stay present in your legal work. Mindfulness can help reduce stress and enhance your ability to make clear, rational decisions. Be aware of your thoughts.

Set Clear Goals

Define your professional and personal goals. The Law of Attraction emphasizes the importance of clarity in what you want to achieve. Write down your goals in a specific, measurable, and time-bound manner.

Visualize Your Success

Spend time each day visualizing the successful outcomes you desire in your legal work. Imagine winning cases, providing excellent legal counsel, and achieving your professional objectives. What do you want in your life? Where do you want to go? See the target. Make it part of your core. Keep it in the forefront of your mind and see you achieving it.

Cultivate an Optimistic Mindset

Replace negative thoughts with positive ones, especially when facing challenges. Focus on solutions and opportunities. Look for the silver linings. When adverse events happen, don't blame yourself. Look for the positive in each situation: What can I learn from this? Although the problem seems harmful, in what way has it helped me? Perhaps you learned patience, strength, courage, or a new route to accomplish your goal.

Use Positive Affirmations

Create positive affirmations related to your legal career and recite them regularly. These affirmations should be in the present tense and reflect your desired outcomes. Daily, write down positive thoughts and beliefs about yourself, better success, who you are, your capability, and the fact that you deserve it.

Stay Patient and Persistent

Recognize that manifesting goals through the Law of Attraction may take time. Be patient and persistent in your efforts, and don't be discouraged by setbacks.

Be Committed

While the Law of Attraction emphasizes the power of intention, it also emphasizes taking inspired action toward your goals. You must proactively work towards your objectives with dedication and perseverance. Thoughts without actions accomplish nothing. Be committed to your plan. Don't let the adverse events stop you. Keep moving forward. Take the steps you need to take to accomplish your desired success.

Seek Guidance

Consider consulting with a mentor who specializes in mindset coaching. They can provide personalized guidance and support, supporting and encouraging you.

Conclusion

While I am unsure whether the Law of Attraction is a scientific reality, the philosophy helps us succeed as we want. There are many things in life you have no control over. But you do control your thoughts and your feelings. They directly impact your actions and your results.

Embracing the potential of the Law of Attraction is like adding an extra dimension to your legal toolkit. By integrating the principles of positive energy, focused intention, and mindful visualization into your practice, you elevate yourself and radiate that positivity outward, shaping the outcomes you seek. The Law of Attraction is not about replacing your legal acumen but amplifying it, infusing your actions with intention, and embracing the profound synergy between the art of law and attraction. Make it work for you.

Key 11: Values Alignment

(Prioritizing Your Values in Your Practice: Why Aligning Your Practice is Key to Building a Successful Career)

"True change happens when you align your heart, truths, and energy."
– Elizabeth Hamilton-Guarino

Do you ever feel unfulfilled by your practice?

Do you struggle with the belief that you're inauthentic in your practice?

Do you ever suffer from burnout?

So many of us have. Often, the problem is that your values need to align with your practice. What if you truly felt your profession was in synergy with your values? What if you were delighted with your practice? What if you started your day feeling motivated and energized? You can create tremendous success and genuine personal freedom by aligning your practice with your values. How do you do that?

This chapter explores why lawyers must align their practice with their most cherished values. We'll unravel the intricacies of this alignment, examining how it not only elevates the legal profession but also transforms lawyers into architects of a more just and compassionate world. Learn the problems you encounter when misaligned.

We detail exactly how to determine your professional values and the gifts from aligning your practice with your values. Finally, access the process for creating a practice aligned with your values.

What Happens if Your Values Don't Align with Your Practice?

When you do not align your practices with your values, you suffer some significant consequences, including:

Lack of Fulfillment

When you do not align with your values, you often feel unfulfilled and dissatisfied with your work, reducing motivation and satisfaction.

Inauthenticity

If you're not true to your values, you often feel like you're living a double life or not being true to yourself. That can lead to a sense of inauthenticity and disconnection from your work. I struggled with that a lot in my earlier career.

Ethical Concerns

If your practice is inconsistent with your values, you may make decisions that conflict with your personal or professional values, leading to ethical concerns and a potential loss of credibility.

Difficulty Building Trust

When your actions conflict with your beliefs, you may find it challenging to build trust with clients and other attorneys, negatively impacting your reputation and ability to succeed.

Burnout

You often experience burnout or other adverse health consequences due to stress, dissatisfaction, or lack of fulfillment when misaligned.

That is a pretty daunting list, isn't it?

How Do You Determine Important Values?

So, what do you do if you want to align your practice with your professional values? Determining your most essential beliefs is a personal process that requires introspection and self-awareness. Here are steps you can take to align your most critical values:

Identify Priorities

Start by identifying the areas of life most important to you, such as family, career, health, spirituality, or community. These priorities guide the identification of values most important to you.

Reflect on Life Experiences

Reflect on past experiences that have been meaningful to you, such as times when you felt proud or fulfilled. Consider what those experiences demonstrated about your values.

Brainstorm Values

Brainstorm a list of values you believe are essential, such as honesty, compassion, justice, fairness, service, or innovation.

Narrow Down the List

Narrow the list of values to the ones that resonate most deeply with you. Then, consider which principles you're willing to sacrifice and which are non-negotiable.

Prioritize Values

Prioritize the values you have identified by ranking them in order of importance. Consider the values most central to your identity and define who you are as a lawyer. You may find that specific values take precedence over others.

Revisit Regularly

Revisit and reassess your values regularly to ensure they align with your priorities and goals.

Adjust and Evolve
Values can evolve. Your priorities and values may change as you gain more experience and encounter different situations. Be open to reevaluating and adjusting your values as needed.

These are some questions you can ask yourself:

- What ethical concerns are non-negotiable?
- Who do I want to represent?
- What kind of person do I want to work with?
- How much money do I want and need to make?
- What do I want my work schedule to be?
- How important is the time I spend with family?
- Do I want to work virtually or in an office?
- How vital are prestige and title?
- What size firm do I want to work in?
- Or do I want to work for the government or in-house?
- How much do I care about independence and autonomy?
- Am I entrepreneurial and want to chart my course?
- Am I interested in serving the public?
- Is social justice an essential value for me?
- Where do I want to live and work?

By asking these questions (and others) and taking these steps, you deepen your understanding of your values and determine what is truly important to you.

Why Is It So Important to Align Your Practice With Your Values?

Aligning your practice with your critical beliefs and goals fosters greater personal freedom in these ways:

Fulfillment
When aligned, you have a true sense of purpose in your work,

which helps you enjoy greater satisfaction.

Authenticity

There is little more important than being true to yourself. You enjoy greater realism and a stronger sense of self. That has been an essential area of growth for me.

Client Relationships

You represent who you want. You strive for the results that fulfill you. As a result, you build stronger relationships with clients because you communicate your beliefs more clearly and authentically.

Motivation

You are more excited about your work and driven to succeed. Your motivation skyrockets because you work towards goals aligned with your fundamental beliefs.

Ethics

Ethical quandaries are less likely to arise when you act according to your personal and professional values; when they do, the solution is more transparent.

Enhanced Job Satisfaction

When your work aligns with your values, you experience a greater career purpose. This satisfaction can lead to increased motivation and enthusiasm in your daily work.

Improved Mental and Emotional Well-Being

Practicing in harmony with one's values can reduce the stress and inner conflict that may arise when facing ethical dilemmas or engaging in work that feels morally conflicting. This can contribute to better mental and emotional health.

You'll enjoy greater personal freedom when this alignment creates greater fulfillment, authenticity, motivation, better client relationships, and tremendous success.

How Do You Align Your Practice With Your Values?

You all want those gifts, don't you? So how do you do it? Here are five steps to create the alignment you all need between your practice and your values:

Determine Your Critical Values

Go through the described process to identify your most important core beliefs and values.

Evaluate Current Practice

Evaluate your current legal practice and determine areas where values are not aligned. For example, if you crave work-life balance but consistently work long hours, you may need to make changes to align your practice with your values better. If independence and autonomy are critical, but you work in a law firm where that is not an option, you should consider an alternative.

Make Changes

Take action to make changes to create synergy between your values and your practice. Consider changes to work habits, such as setting boundaries around working hours, taking regular breaks, or changing the types of clients or cases taken. Or, you may need to look for a different firm or type of legal endeavor.

Communicate Values

Communicate your critical values to your colleagues, clients, and associates. As a result, you'll build trust and establish a reputation for ethical behavior when you transparently communicate your beliefs.

Seek Guidance from Mentors

Connect with experienced mentors or colleagues who share your values or have successfully aligned their practice with their principles. They can provide valuable guidance and insights. They can also help you make changes and stay aligned with your values. Support can provide accountability, guidance, and encouragement.

Re-evaluate Regularly

Re-evaluate your values and practice regularly to ensure they remain aligned with your values. Reflect on cases, decisions, and interactions that challenged your principles, and consider how you can better align your actions with your values moving forward. This evaluation will identify areas for improvement and ensure that you stay on track with your goals and values.

Aligning your legal practice with your values is an ongoing journey. It may involve making tough choices and navigating ethical gray areas, but it is essential for maintaining professional integrity and personal fulfillment as a lawyer. Ultimately, your values should serve as a guiding compass in your legal career, helping you make decisions that resonate with your core principles.

Conclusion

In conclusion, aligning your law practice with your values is an ethical and strategic choice. This alignment is an aspiration and a profound commitment to the principles that define you. It can help you build stronger client relationships, enhance your reputation, and increase your job satisfaction. But most importantly, it allows you to make a meaningful contribution to the legal profession and society. You become a powerful force for positive change when you stand up for your beliefs and act by your values. So, if you haven't already, take some time to reflect on your values and how they can inform your legal practice. Your clients, colleagues, and conscience will thank you for it. As you navigate your legal journey, may your values be the North Star that guides you toward a successful, significant, and ethically resplendent practice.

Key 12: Mentorship

(THE MENTORSHIP ADVANTAGE: WHY EVERY LAWYER NEEDS A GUIDE)

"A mentor is someone who sees more talent and ability within you than you see in yourself and helps bring it out of you."
– Bob Proctor

Have you ever felt confused or lost?

Or trying to figure out how to get there?

Have you felt frustrated and wondered why?

Have you felt stressed?

Would it be good to ask for support, but you need to figure out who or how to ask?

Do you ever wish you had someone to chat with?

To answer your questions?

To listen to you empathetically?

What if you were no longer overwhelmed by stress?

What if you had the clarity to know where you wanted to go and exactly how to get there?

What if you could be successful, fulfilled, and delighted?

**What if you had someone at your beck and call
who was always there to listen to you confidentially
and support and encourage you?**

Feeling lost, trapped, confused, and alone is not unusual. Most of us have felt that way at times. You know you need help and guidance but are afraid to ask for it. The journey from a law school graduate to a seasoned legal professional can be challenging and daunting. However, there's a source of guidance that can illuminate this path and make the voyage far less treacherous: mentorship. Whether you're a fresh-faced law school graduate just embarking on your legal career or a seasoned attorney looking to refine your skills and chart a course to leadership, the benefits of lawyers seeking support from a mentor are immeasurable.

In this chapter, I share my varied experiences with mentorship, explain why it is difficult to ask for support, and discuss the gifts of obtaining the guidance you deserve. We explore the profound advantages of mentorship, offering invaluable insights into how this dynamic relationship can shape your career, foster personal growth, and ultimately lead to legal excellence. Join me on this journey of discovery and unveiling the transformative power of mentorship.

My Experience with Mentorship

I have learned the benefits of receiving the right coaching from the right person at the right time. My dad had always been my mentor. He was constantly supportive, providing loving guidance, and always there for me. There was an absolute emptiness when he passed because he was one person I always turned to for support.

I have been an avid golfer my whole life. I played for my high school team and my college team. By now, I have played for over 55 years. I should understand the sport perfectly well by now. But beginning when I was 13, I have always had a golf pro who coached me in the game. I have had a golf coach every year since, including now. While I understand the game, I seldom perceive what I need to do better or where I am off track. That coaching helps me know how to improve, play better, and have more confidence and fun.

My brother, Gene, who became an attorney eight years before me, guided me throughout my legal career. He advised me about my career, networking, handling cases, knowledge of local judges and lawyers, and much more. He was one of the most highly respected attorneys in our area.

I began my journey in sobriety over 30 years ago. Not only did I struggle with addiction to alcohol, but my thinking was way out of balance. I was full of self-centeredness, shame, and guilt. I have always had a sponsor who has helped me to understand how to live life sober and to change my ways of acting and living. Now, I see reality as it is, and I respond appropriately. My sponsor helps me to live life on life's terms. It has indeed been invaluable.

More recently, I entered a new field in my practice of law. I had always been a very successful personal injury trial attorney, primarily on the defense side. However, 15 years ago, I embarked on a new career as a family law attorney. I wanted to be of more direct and personal help to my clients. I was insecure and uncomfortable, knowing very little about that area of law. A fellow attorney whom I had known for some years became my mentor. He provided me with forms, told me about the critical cases in the most important areas, and answered numerous questions about handling my client's unique situation. When I was stuck, he helped me. I am very grateful to him for the service he has provided to me. He has helped me become an independent, confident, highly regarded family law attorney.

These experiences have taught me the excellent benefits of having a coach who supports us on our journey. Yet, it's often hard to ask for the help you need.

The Difficulty in Asking for Support

Why is it so hard to ask for help? Primarily, it's out of fear. You may know you could benefit from the guidance of an independent third party, but you're simply afraid to ask. In law practice, you learn to be confident, independent, competent, and in charge. The thought that you may need help conflicts with your identity as an attorney. You worry that others will see you as weak or incompetent. Today's culture honors self-help and independence. The fear of seeking help will undermine your confidence, make you question your abilities, or create anxiety.

Sometimes, you need to be self-aware enough to know that some coaching would be helpful to you. But, more importantly, even when you do, you're afraid of how you might look if you ask someone for help. Of course, those feelings, while natural and understandable, are not accurate. No one thinks less of us when we ask for help. You should never let that unwarranted fear stop you from obtaining the support you need.

Here are some of the significant roadblocks to lawyers seeking support from a mentor:

Perceived Self-Sufficiency

Lawyers must be self-reliant and independent problem solvers. You should have all the answers and handle challenges independently, making it difficult to ask for assistance. So, how could you need help?

Fear of Vulnerability

Lawyers project confidence and expertise, and there may be a fear of appearing vulnerable or inexperienced when seeking guidance from a mentor.

Ego and Pride

Some lawyers have solid egos and take pride in their abilities. Asking for help can be seen as admitting weakness or inadequacy, which can be challenging to overcome.

Time Constraints

Lawyers often have demanding work schedules and may worry

that mentorship will be time-consuming. This concern about time constraints can discourage them from seeking support.

Lack of Awareness
Some lawyers may need to fully understand the benefits of mentorship or recognize their need for guidance. This lack of awareness can be a significant roadblock.

Overestimation of Knowledge
Lawyers may overestimate their knowledge and skills, believing they already know everything they need to succeed. This overconfidence can prevent them from recognizing the value of mentorship.

Financial Concerns
Lawyers may need to learn the costs involved or see the return on investment a mentor can provide.

Lawyers should recognize that seeking mentorship is a sign of strength and a commitment to professional growth. You don't have all the answers. Lack of time and money are stories you tell yourself to justify not getting the support you need. Don't let fear or ego get in your way. It's important to remember that even the most accomplished lawyers have sought guidance and support at various points in their careers.

How Can A Mentor Benefit A Lawyer?

Do you know how you often feel you have no want to talk to? Knowing to is for advice? Or the support and accountability you need? These are some of the ways a mentor can benefit you:

A Confidential Listening Ear
You feel so alone sometimes, don't you? You may be afraid to talk to your partner, coworkers, law school classmates, or even your spouse or family. You do not want to appear weak or be judged for your

feelings or struggles. Mentors can be very effective, confidential, and supportive listeners. Your mentor will always be there to hear you and to understand.

Guidance

Often, you need to figure out what to do next. You're still determining where to turn or how to get there. Your mentor has many years of experience and can give helpful suggestions about your goals.

Vision Creation

Sometimes, your mentor sees your abilities and future that you do not see in yourself. I know I've experienced that with my clients. I have a vision of how incredible their future can be, but they have not yet seen it. Your mentor can help you create a vision for your future that may be more powerful than you know for yourself.

Clarity

Sometimes, you feel like you're in a fog, confused. Your mentor can clarify where you are, where you want to get to, and how to get there.

Confidence

Your mentor is always on your side, lifting, encouraging, and supporting. He affirms your talents and your positive traits. An ongoing mentorship process helps you develop self-confidence and resilience to overcome challenges.

Accountability

Sometimes, the same mistakes keep happening; you back away from the same hurdles or are afraid to take the next steps. Your mentor can hold you accountable. Together, you can set targets for your next task, and your mentor will encourage you to meet those goals and deadlines you set for yourself.

What Are the Essential Criteria In Selecting A Mentor?

When selecting a mentor, you should use great care in selecting just the right mentor. These are some of the factors you may consider:

Experience
How much experience does the mentor have as an attorney and a coach? Has he experienced many of the same things that you have? It's essential to find a mentor who has the background and experience so that they truly can understand and advise you.

Good Listener
Engaging in a relationship with the mentor can create a sense of vulnerability. It's an open and honest relationship. The client shares personal information with the mentor. For that reason, the mentor must be a good listener and empathetic.

Compatibility
The most critical factor in selecting a mentor is compatibility. You should "click" with your mentor. The mentor listens to and speaks with you in ways that make you feel comfortable and encouraged. Personal compatibility is crucial. Seek a mentor with whom you have a good rapport and shared values. A positive and respectful relationship will foster effective mentorship.

What Are Some Of The Gifts Of Getting The Support You Need?

The benefits can be incredible when you become aware that you need some coaching and ask for it. The goals you set for yourself are now more easily achievable, and your path to accomplishing your vision is more apparent. These are some of the tangible gifts of accepting coaching:

Long-Term Relationships

Mentorship often leads to lasting professional relationships. Over time, mentees may become mentors, passing on knowledge and experiences to the next generation of lawyers. Sharing yourself transparently, seeking their assistance, listening to their guidance, and growing professionally create an exceptional relationship. You've become more open, and the mentor appreciates that. Your coach appreciates both your openness and the opportunity to be of support. It creates a common bond that is unique and special.

Motivation and Inspiration

A mentor can inspire and motivate lawyers to reach their full potential. Success and encouragement can fuel determination and perseverance.

Greater Resilience

Without support, you're fragile and uncertain. You don't have a sense of direction or how to overcome your obstacles. With proper coaching, you begin to facilitate your personal growth and development. As a result, you become more resilient, know how to overcome your setbacks, and obtain guidance to continue growing.

Growth Mindset

You break out of the thinking pattern, "I am not good at that," or "This is a task that is beyond me." Our performance improves. You grow and expand. You can achieve things that previously seemed impossible to us. You can improve and learn what you need to accomplish your goals.

Emotional Stability

You're no longer fragile. You connect with a coach who helps you understand what is happening and how to handle it. As a result, your confidence and self-awareness grow. You are no longer isolated and filled with worry and doubt. You have the support you need and know who to turn to when you need guidance.

Reducing Isolation

The legal profession can sometimes be isolating, with lawyers working on complex cases independently. You are each in your silo. A mentor provides a support system and a sounding board, reducing feelings of professional isolation. You no longer feel so alone.

Personal Growth

Mentorship extends beyond professional development. Mentors often share life lessons, imparting wisdom that helps lawyers grow as individuals and make well-rounded life choices. Your mentor shares knowledge and experience that allows us to understand your circumstances better.

Constructive Feedback

Mentors offer constructive criticism and feedback. They help you identify strengths and weaknesses, encouraging continuous improvement and growth.

Confidence Boost

Having a mentor who believes in your abilities can boost your self-confidence. This emotional support is precious during challenging times or when tackling new and unfamiliar legal challenges.

Greater Success

You achieve clarity about your work. You're more confident and resilient. A new vision of your future fuels you. You know how to accomplish your goals. You have answers to the questions that confused you. With more wisdom, understanding, and confidence, you achieve tremendous success and freedom.

You deserve these gifts!

Conclusion

The journey to success is not a solitary endeavor. It's a dynamic path that requires continuous growth, adaptability, and the pursuit of excellence. The journey is easier when a lawyer embraces the transformative power of coaching. A coach is your dedicated partner in your professional development, helping you harness your full potential, refine your skills, and achieve your loftiest goals.

You'll overcome obstacles with a coach and chart a course to greatness with unwavering determination. You should never let your fear or ego stop you from seeking the support you need. Instead, let a coach propel you toward a future of unparalleled success and fulfillment.

The choice is clear: your journey will be smoother and more successful with a coach as your trusted guide and ally.

Final Thoughts

On my podcast, *The Free Lawyer*, I often pose a pivotal question to my guests: "What words of wisdom would you offer to a lawyer, confined to their office, wrestling with stress, overwhelmed, and teetering on the brink of burnout?" Their responses, filled with profound insights, have illuminated the way forward for many.

Yet, today, the spotlight turns to me. I'm acutely aware of the legal profession's formidable challenges. From difficult clients to demanding colleagues, the billable hour treadmill, the relentless pursuit of success, and the unrelenting workload, you face stressors that can make the practice of law an uphill battle. The hours can be long, and the pressure can become almost suffocating.

All too frequently, I engage with lawyers who fondly remember the jubilation of passing the bar exam—a monumental achievement in their legal journey, celebrated with enthusiasm and high hopes for their new profession. However, as the years pass, a sense of disillusionment creeps in. Three, five, or ten years down the road, they question why they became lawyers in the first place. The reality doesn't align with their expectations. Stress, frustration, and a profound sense of unfulfillment take hold.

So, what guidance can I offer these lawyers facing the abyss? It's a formidable challenge, but within this closing chapter, we will explore ten transformative tips that can rekindle the spark for those on the brink of quitting, toiling away in solitude.

Remember:

You're Never Alone

It's easy to feel isolated in the midst of turmoil. Yet, you must remember you're not alone in this struggle. Countless lawyers, perhaps even the one in the neighboring office, grapple with the same pressures. This shared experience can be a source of comfort and solidarity.

It Doesn't Have to Be This Way

When the darkness looms, it's essential to cling to hope. Possibilities illuminate the path to a fulfilling and successful legal practice. It doesn't have to remain a dilemma of stress; change is possible.

There's Always a Solution

Even when the burden seems unbearable, believe this truth: solutions exist. The answer may seem elusive, but trust that you can uncover a path to fulfillment and freedom.

You're Never Stuck

The legal profession offers a multitude of avenues where you can apply your skills and knowledge. You're not tethered to your current role; you can shape your legal journey within your current firm or elsewhere.

Define Your Core Values

Understanding the source of your frustration is the first step towards change. What aspects of your current situation weigh you down? Is it a longing for independence, a thirst for a different work environment, or a passion for a specific area of law? Identifying your core values opens the door to positive transformation.

Seek Fulfillment

Remember why you chose to become a lawyer in the first place.

Most attorneys embark on this journey with a deep-seated desire to make a positive impact, serve the underprivileged, and improve society. Rediscover that sense of fulfillment by aligning your practice with your core values. When passion guides your work, stress and overwhelm fade, replaced by purpose.

Be Present

Focusing on the here and now is crucial in a distracted world. Engage fully in your conversations, tasks, and interactions. Transformation occurs in the present moment, and you can find happiness and joy.

Practice Acceptance

Learn to let go of the things you cannot change, such as the behavior of others or uncontrollable circumstances. Redirect your focus toward your thoughts, feelings, and actions. Accepting what you cannot change grants you greater freedom.

Cultivate Gratitude

Amidst the stress, remember the countless things to be thankful for: your health, financial security, and the privilege of belonging to a noble profession. Embrace an attitude of gratitude, and many of your stressors will lose their grip on you.

Seek Support

Surround yourself with friends who genuinely care and support you. Stay connected with them and lean on them when needed. Find a wise mentor who can provide guidance, encouragement, and accountability. With a support system in place, you're never truly alone in your journey.

In your quest to transform stress into success, remember that change is possible, and a fulfilling legal career is within your grasp. Embrace these ten tips as your guiding light on this transformative journey.

So, for that lawyer who once questioned their path, remember this: you can reshape your legal career, redefine your purpose, and turn stress into a stepping stone toward a brighter, more fulfilling future. Your journey to success begins now.

In Closing

Let me close with this letter to you,
expressing my wishes for you;

Dear Friend.

Thank you for taking the time to enjoy Breaking Free. I am glad you chose to explore how to achieve a personal freedom you did not think possible.

Breaking Free is not a book to read and just think about logically as we often do as lawyers. Instead, applying these tools is an experience, transformational steps we try to utilize daily. The tools are only as helpful as we work them.

I know with the clients I have coached that when they apply these tools in their daily lives, they feel lighter, more peaceful, more free. You can enjoy a level of happiness and contentment you did not think possible.

There is a lot of material in Breaking Free. Try to implement the 12 keys one piece at a time. Make a goal to utilize the tools daily. With focus and effort, you can truly change your life. The stresses you experience as a lawyer will always be there. How you manage them, how you think about them, and what you focus on can be indeed life-changing.

We develop patterns and habits over many years, and changing them is difficult. I played golf since I was 13 and have had a golf coach each year since for 55 years. I know what a good golf swing looks like. I know what I am supposed to do. But I don't know what I'm doing right and what I'm doing wrong, what needs to be changed, and how to make that change. My golf coach helps me.

Applying these steps and making these fundamental changes is difficult and often requires a second set of experienced eyes.

If you need support in making changes to achieve the true personal freedom you deserve, I'm always here to support you. You may reach out to me at any time. I am passionate about helping you achieve the life you always dreamed of. I am here to help you.

For now, please be well, be safe, and be free.

Wishing you all the best,
Gary
www.garymiles.net
gary@garymiles.net

About The Author

Gary Miles is a legal luminary with over four decades of experience practicing law, primarily in litigation and family law. His journey through the legal landscape has been marked by diverse roles, including that of a trial lawyer, managing partner, author, leader, and entrepreneur. His passion for helping individuals navigate the complexities of their lives led him to a unique path as a success coach for lawyers.

Having witnessed the relentless pressures that lawyers face in the legal profession, Gary has dedicated his life to guiding his clients toward fulfillment in their practice. His practical tools and empathetic approach have empowered countless legal professionals to overcome their mindset blocks and break free from the prisons that once limited their potential.

Breaking Free: A Guide to Achieving Personal and Professional Freedom as a Lawyer reflects Gary's commitment to the legal community. In this transformative book, he distills his extensive knowledge into 12 prisons of the mind and 12 keys to unlock those prisons. With a profound understanding of lawyers' challenges, Gary empowers readers to find contentment, success, and freedom within their law practice.

Gary's legacy is one of resilience, wisdom, and unwavering dedication to helping lawyers thrive in their careers and lives. Through his writing, coaching, and leadership, he continues to inspire legal professionals to unlock their full potential and experience the freedom they deserve.

You can find Gary at www.garymiles.net, or contact him at gary@garymiles.net.

About The Book

*In Breaking Free: A Guide to Achieving Personal
and Professional Freedom as a Lawyer,*

Gary Miles invites you on a transformative journey. This book is a compass for those seeking contentment, success, and freedom within their law practice. It is written by a legal sage with over four decades of experience.

The legal world often feels like a maze of challenges, pressures, and limitations. Gary Miles, drawing from his wealth of knowledge as a trial lawyer, managing partner, and success coach, has distilled the essence of these challenges into 12 prisons of the mind. These prisons represent the mental barriers that can hold lawyers back from reaching their full potential, both personally and professionally.

But "Breaking Free" doesn't merely focus on the problems. It is a guide to liberation, offering 12 keys to unlock these mental prisons. Gary's compassionate and practical approach provides lawyers with the tools and insights to overcome their mindset blocks and break free from the constraints that have held them captive.

This book is not just a collection of words on paper; it's a roadmap to a more fulfilling legal practice and life. Whether you're struggling with imposter syndrome, battling perfectionism, or feeling overwhelmed by the demands of the legal profession, Gary Miles offers guidance, support, and a path to personal and professional growth.

Breaking Free is a testament to Gary's dedication to helping lawyers find contentment, success, and freedom. It's a message of hope for those who want to rediscover their passion for law and reignite the joy in their practice. So, if you're ready to embark on a journey of self-discovery, transformation, and ultimate freedom, this book is your trusted companion on that path. Unlock the doors to your success and fulfillment today with "Breaking Free."

"Gary Miles is not just a lawyer with over 40+ years of experience; he is, more importantly, a dear friend of mine. His knowledge and expertise of the law profession and all it encompasses makes him an expert in his space. When I first heard his incredible podcast, "The Free Lawyer," on iTunes, I said, "This guy needs to write a book!". And guess what? He did!

In his first book, " Breaking Free – A Guide To Achieve Personal and Professional Freedom As A Lawyer," you will learn precisely what Gary has done to create a harmonious balance of work, family, and life. If you are a law professional struggling to find that balance, look no further. This book is for you, and I couldn't recommend it enough."

– Scott Aaron. Co-Founder of
The Time To Grow and Expert Authority Mastermind

"Gary is an amazing expert in his field, with over 40+ years as an attorney. His passion for helping lawyers to live their best lives shines through in this book. This is the ultimate guide for lawyers who want to improve their lives professionally and personally. Gary shares terrific insights, and reading it feels like having a heart-to-heart with a mentor who understands lawyers' struggles. Grabbing a copy is a no-brainer if you're in the legal field. It's packed with advice that can totally change the game for you! It is a must-read!

– Nancy Evans, CEO of BYOB Agency

"Gary provides an essential voice of progress in the legal space. Gary's willingness to selflessly provide sage guidance and pragmatic wisdom

on how lawyers can thrive, instead of merely survive, in their careers makes him invaluable to the profession."

– Wendy Merrill, law firm
consultant and CEO of StrategyHorse

"Gary has the gift of bringing out the best in you as an attorney, but he also gets you to identify and harness your strengths. Not only does he offer his business expertise, but he is also in touch with what makes human beings as productive and successful as possible. If you get the chance to learn from him, consider yourself extremely fortunate. I certainly do."

– Sara Kaplan-Khodorovsky, Esq

www.ingramcontent.com/pod-product-compliance
Lightning Source LLC
Chambersburg PA
CBHW070925260726
48661CB00003B/832